Activity-based management

Activity-based management

New approaches to measuring performance and managing costs

Edited by **Michael Morrow**
with contributions from
>Alan Bainbridge
Tim Connolly
Alistair Gray
Martin Hazell
Mike Jeans
Neil Malcolm
Ketan Patel
Peter Scott

Woodhead-Faulkner

New York   London   Toronto   Sydney   Tokyo   Singapore

First published 1992 by
Woodhead-Faulkner
Campus 400, Maylands Avenue
Hemel Hempstead
Hertfordshire, HP2 7EZ
A division of
Simon & Schuster International Group

Disc conversion in 10/12 pt Plantin
by Columns Typesetters of Reading

Printed and bound in Great Britain by
BPC Wheatons Ltd, Exeter

British Library Cataloguing in Publication Data

A catalogue record for this book is available from the
British Library

ISBN 0–85941–7751 (hbk)

---

3   4   5   96   95   94

✓ = Worth Reading

Contents

v

Acknowledgements

As management consultants our role is to understand new thinking in our chosen area and turn such ideas and developments into practical solutions which benefit our clients. For this reason our book makes many references to the work of others. It would be entirely inappropriate, however, to leave two of these names, Robin Cooper and Robert Kaplan, as footnotes. The effect their work has had on the development of approaches to performance measurement and cost management throughout the world cannot be underestimated. Through sharing their ideas with us, we have benefited greatly and we wish to acknowledge this.

Acknowledgement is also due to Carol Lawrence and Sue Nickells for their great help in preparing the manuscript and graphics for this book.

List of Abbreviations

ABC	=	activity-based costing
AGV	=	automated guided vehicle
AMT	=	advanced manufacturing technology
AQL	=	acceptable quality level
ASRS	=	automated storage and retrieval system
AVCO	=	average costing
CAD	=	computer automated design
CAM-I	=	Computer Aided Manufacturing International
CIM	=	computer integrated manufacturing
CMS	=	cost management system
CNC	=	computer numerical control
CSF	=	critical success factor
DNC	=	direct numerical control
DPP	=	direct product profitability
EDI	=	electronic data interchange
EIS	=	executive information system
FIFO	=	first-in-first-out
FMS	=	flexible manufacturing system
GT	=	group technology
IBAS	=	intelligent body assembly system
JIT	=	just-in-time
LIFO	=	last-in-first-out
MCR	=	management control reporting
MIS	=	management information system
MRP	=	material requirements planning
MRP2	=	manufacturing resource planning
MTBF	=	mean time between failure
NIC	=	newly industrialised country
NIFO	=	next-in-first-out
NPI	=	new product introduction

NTED = no-touch exchange of dies
OPT   = optimised production technology
OTED = one-touch exchange of dies
PBB   = priority-based budgeting
PBT   = profit before tax
PPV   = purchase price variance
ROCE = return on capital employed
SMED = single-minute exchange of dies
TQM   = total quality management
VFM   = value for money
WIP   = work-in-progress

Introduction

There can be very few managers concerned with performance measurement and cost management who have not by now come across some reference to activity-based approaches, whether given the label of activity-based costing, activity accounting or the wider term we have adopted for this book, activity-based management. Many will have read articles or attended conferences on the subject. Without doubt, activity-based management has become the most talked about subject in management accounting for many years. Why should this be? Why should a technique which started as a way of recalculating overheads for product costing have caused so much stir and interest?

The answer is that the emergence of activity-based approaches has triggered a latent dissatisfaction with the way many businesses go about measuring performance and managing costs. The essential point about activity-based approaches is that they represent a return to reflecting reality in the way management information is compiled and reported. Instead of arbitrary cost allocations, complex cross-charging and meaningless variance analysis, activity-based approaches are mostly applied common-sense – giving visibility to what is happening in the business. It is this return to clarity and usefulness which makes activity-based approaches so attractive and has caused a ripple effect to widen their range of applications and the use of the underlying philosophy.

Whilst activity-based approaches are by no means a universal panacea, nor even an end in themselves, they do at least recognise the obvious – that to be effective managers have to manage the activities that make up the business, and the way costs are reported and performance measures are set should reflect this.

The structure of this book follows the development of new approaches to measuring performance and managing costs. The first chapter therefore describes the great changes which have transformed the manufacturing sector in recent years in so many ways and which

1

represent, perhaps, just the first phase of ever greater changes which we are only now beginning to appreciate. The second and third chapters describe how many traditional approaches to measuring performance and managing costs have become of less use and from this how activity-based approaches developed. The following chapters describe the application of activity-based approaches and place them in the wider context of providing information for use by management; namely product costing, profitability analysis, budgeting and cost reporting, operational control, performance measurement and process improvement. This structure reinforces the point made earlier that activity-based approaches are a means to an end, rather than being an end in themselves, and should become, where appropriate, an integral part of providing management information to improve business performance.

The final chapter is concerned with the practical and systems issues which surround making improvements to measuring performance and managing costs more effectively.

Finally, no introduction of this nature would be complete without a quote, and this one serves to make the point, if it is needed, that the issues raised in this book are not really new at all:

'Reports and procedures should focus only on the performance needed to achieve results in the key areas. To control everything is to control nothing. And to attempt to control the irrelevant always misdirects.' (*The Practice of Management*, Peter F. Drucker, 1954)

CHAPTER 1

The new manufacturing environment

The purpose of this chapter is to provide an insight into some of the current pressures and opportunities in manufacturing industries as a background to considering performance measurement and cost management issues. After reflecting on some of the essential characteristics of the current worldwide competitive situation, the main forces behind the many recent changes in the sector are examined and a number of key philosophies, including total quality management, just-in-time and simultaneous engineering, are discussed. Finally, some of the current technologies which have enabled significant advances in manufacturing effectiveness to take place are reviewed.

Global competition

Global competition has intensified in the last ten years and is likely to escalate at an increasing rate in the future. The pattern is not new but the rate of change is. The late twentieth century is a time in which the number of companies taking an ever-more global perspective has risen steadily. Takeovers, mergers, strategic alliances, joint venture agreements and straightforward competitive success from organic growth have consolidated the position of world-class, global companies. Now, more than ever before, companies must compete with the best in the world – even in their own domestic markets.

Figure 1.1 represents the trend of globalisation as organisations have worked towards a situation in which, today, the world must be treated as a single, integrated market. In the 1920s and 1930s, for example, European firms were content to allow their individual country subsidiaries to pursue their own strategies without imposing the home nation's policies. Indicative of the second phase is the situation in the United States during the 1960s, for example, in which US corporations

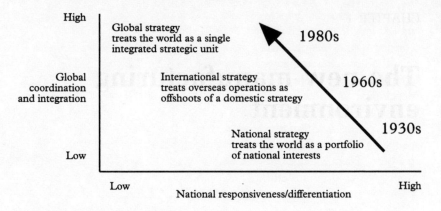

Figure 1.1 The trend of globalisation. Source: Professor Sumantra Ghoshal (1990), INSEAD, Paris.

tended to regard their overseas operations as offshoots of a US domestic strategy.

In many sectors, corporate globalisation has brought about conditions in which profits are coming under increasing pressure. In Europe, cosy domestic markets have been broken down by the Single European Market together with the redrawing of the boundaries of Western economic influence in Eastern Europe and the break-up of what was the Soviet Union. Manufacturing companies from the newly industrialised countries (NIC), such as Korea, have been battling for international competitiveness, founded on world-class performance, right from the outset. The threat to Western companies from the NICs is now a reality.

Clearly there are barriers – protectionism, local content levels, quotas and technology transfer restrictions – but these cannot stem the tide of global influence indefinitely. Increasingly, businesses must invest time and resources to understand political, socioeconomic and environmental conditions as a prerequisite to establishing a successful global enterprise.[1]

Competitive power is being concentrated in fewer companies and these multinationals must work hard to match the wish to empower local management with the need to maintain a common thread that ties the corporation together, sustaining and protecting the fabric of competitive strength. Sony Corporation[2] has stated that the global deployment of capital, human and organisational resources is an essential requirement to compete in today's markets. The evolution of Sony's management system can be summarised as a process of delegating operational control as activities spread over the world, and simultaneously fortifying central strategic coordination and control to meet global competition.

A term used by NEC Corporation[3] is 'mesh-globalisation'. It describes frameworks within which people, capital, products and technologies move frequently between the company's overseas affiliates. NEC considers the people or human resource issues as preeminent in successfully competing at a global level against its international competitors. It believes one of the critical issues is recognising, developing and rewarding managerial talent.

The new manufacturing environment is therefore one in which there is not only a brisk international trade in products and technologies, but in people who must be adaptable. Personal mobility, flexibility in being ready to accept change and the ability to succeed within the constraints imposed by corporate culture, are all factors in which individuals will have the opportunity to prosper.

Competitive strategy

In most sectors of manufacturing industry, international competition has signalled an end to a situation in which customers could be relied upon to look no further than the latest catalogue of derivative products with their planned obsolescence and long delivery times. Customers are now more exacting and are ready to buy from anywhere. They look for innovative products which are more reliable, instantly available and sell at the right price.

From the market perspective, the inherent dynamics of competition within industries have been thoroughly explored. Michael Porter, in his seminal work on competitive advantage,[4] states that this advantage grows fundamentally out of the value a firm is able to create for the buyers of its products and services. His 'value chain' model (Figure 1.2) disaggregates the company under scrutiny into the discrete but interrelated activities from which value stems. The value chain can then be related to **external** competitive pressures and a view of the structure of the **whole** industry sector. This view comprises suppliers to the industry, its customers, players in the industry, potential new entrants and alternative products. From this view, a business can decide the nature of its competitive advantage and how this can be sustained.

The place of 'manufacturing' in corporate strategy and the need to incorporate manufacturing process considerations as a key element in the total picture are topics explored by Terry Hill in his book, *Manufacturing Strategy*.[5] The central questions asked are what are the qualifying criteria for being in the market and what are the criteria that actually win orders. A generic list of these order-winning and qualifying criteria (Table 1.1)

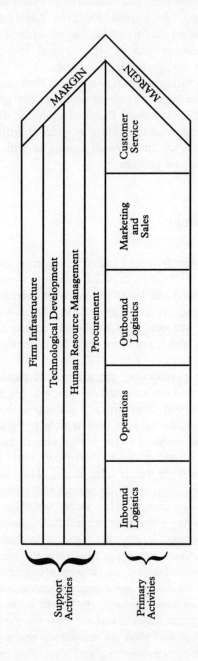

Figure 1.2 The value chain developed by Michael Porter.[4]

shows that they fall readily into three categories: price, fitness for use and service. Table 1.1 shows the specific criteria for two simple products.

Product quality and consistency are essential for a supplier of saline solution to hospitals. It is, however, the company's ability to deliver

Table 1.1 Order-winning and qualifying criteria.

Generic criteria		Product/market-specific criteria	
		Example: saline solution	Example: mineral water
Price	Purchase price Delivery cost	Price	Price
Fitness for use	Product specification Consistency of analysis	Qualifier: product quality and consistency	Qualifier: product purity Taste
	Appearance of packaging Durability Tamper protection/seals	Quality of packaging	
Service Before:	Technical assistance Flexibility on labelling Packaging options		
During:	Lead-time Delivery reliability Delivery accuracy Volume/mix flexibility	Delivery accuracy and reliability	
After:	Technical/ marketing support Replacement service Information support	Unconditional replacement guarantee	Delivery service

exactly what is ordered, when it is wanted that wins orders. With many products, new innovations can change a quality qualifier into an order winner and sometimes, as Perrier discovered, failing in a qualifier can be disastrous. Perrier's manufacturing efficiency had enabled them to produce 1.2 billion bottles in 1989 but flaws in the quality assurance part of their manufacturing process produced well-known and disastrous results in 1990.[6]

Determining the 'order-winning criteria' is therefore a critical step both in determining what is important in manufacturing strategy and in providing the focus to guide many of the day-to-day decisions within a company.

With a clear view of customers' expectations and spurred on by the risk of losing market share to domestic and multiplying foreign competitors, manufacturing businesses must recognise increasingly the importance of working together as a team. This will frequently mean developing performance improvement projects which demand coordinated action from all functions. A simple example is the bringing together of sales and production management in the introduction of a master production schedule to balance plant resources whilst maintaining customer service levels. Such action, if not already in place, can be hugely effective.

Time-based competition

It is useful to summarise the effect on manufacturing of the new global environment by describing five crucial areas of opportunity. Four of the five are time-based opportunities and these new 'time-based imperatives' are the central themes of many initiatives to improve competitiveness in the 1990s:

● **Reducing time-to-market for new product introductions**: The significance of this step in many companies and its relationship with decreasing product life cycles make it a prime candidate for the top five. The emphasis on time-to-market through collapsing product life cycles is explored further later in this chapter.

● **Reducing manufacturing lead-time**: Manufacturing lead-time, or cycle-time as it is called in the United States, is the elapsed period between commitment to buy the longest lead-time input material and completion of the finished product. Colossal disparity is often found between total manufacturing lead-time and the length of time on which the product is actually being worked.

There are many case studies demonstrating companies' success in cutting manufacturing lead-times:[7] Hewlett Packard in one plant sliced it from 22 days to only 1 day and as a result cut inventory holding space by half, production costs by one-third and distribution space by nearly a quarter. Omark Industries has cut manufacturing lead-time from 21 to 3 days enabling it to convert from a make-to-stock environment based on a forecast, to a make-to-order.

- **Reducing customer lead-time**: This is the period of time from when the customer requests an order to when it is delivered. Through a combination of getting closer to the customer, understanding the needs **early** and building this information into the forecasting process, innovative product-building techniques can be employed. Modularisation and redesigning products so they can be configured at the last moment to precise customer requirements is a key method by which performance in this area can be improved.

- **Reducing process changeover time**: The benefits from cutting process changeover times can be huge in relation to the effort required. Increasingly, companies are realising that focusing on this precise area can pay enormous dividends. Toyota is obsessive in its attention to reducing changeover times and their terminology, now universally used, emphasises the progressive path to eliminating the time altogether. Single-minute exchange of dies (SMED) represents a sub-ten minute change, a stage on the way to one-touch exchange of dies (OTED) and finally no-touch exchange of dies (NTED). Cutting changeover time in all processes is a cornerstone of just-in-time philosophy and is possibly the most rapid route to making significant reductions in production batch sizes, thereby achieving manufacturing flexibility.

- **Stabilising schedules**: Effective synchronisation is essential to the production element of manufacturing so that tasks are carried out to plan with dates for internal 'delivery' at each stage. Delivering early may be just as disruptive as delivering late. For example, handling raw materials and components delivered early wastes space and effort. Also, the early ones may arrive at the expense of others which are late. Being able to plan and rely on a scheduled date produces enormous benefits throughout the whole manufacturing process. It should be emphasised that creating a stable schedule is more than just forcing suppliers to deliver on time. All internal processes should strive to achieve it too; such as adhering rigorously to the production schedule on the shopfloor and having sales and marketing improve their selling forecast. The instability injected into a company by failing to meet the forecast at product line level is rarely recognised.

Product life cycles

The explosion in the rate of technological innovation means that product life cycles are collapsing. Shorter product life cycles affect every industry; Figure 1.3 illustrates this, comparing the position 50 years ago with today.

Companies must now make decisions more quickly and speed up the rate at which they introduce new products to the market. The vice chairman of Peripherals Incorporated, a US electronics company, summed up the impact: 'The first guy to market cleans up, the second guy does OK and the third guy barely breaks even – the fourth guy loses money.'

Shorter life cycles shift the emphasis of competitive strength and value-added away from production and the consumption of cost in material and labour in manufacture, towards the judgements made and costs incurred **before** production. Rapid and efficient design processes and life-cycle-based cost planning are therefore essential in the new environment.

Figure 1.4 illustrates the consequence on life cycle profit in the electronics industry, from delayed introduction to the marketplace. McKinsey found that being late-to-market was ten times worse than spending 50% more during the development process.

In many products it is typical that as much as 65% of the cost of the product is determined during the design process with a further 20% being influenced by the configuration of the manufacturing facilities

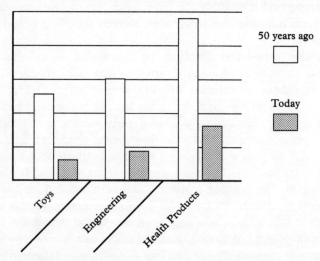

Figure 1.3   The pressure on life cycles.

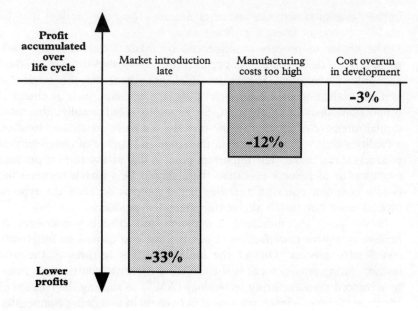

Figure 1.4 Life cycle profits.

themselves. The remaining 15% is all that is left to be controlled by direct manufacturing management. For cost management, influencing design and development early on is where the real advantage is won. This point is returned to in Chapter 4 'Product costing'.

Some large corporations actually plan for a high mortality rate for the ideas coming out of their product concept and design teams. One of the great challenges is to inspire designers to be innovative and at the same time keep fundamental changes to the product to a minimum. This incremental innovation concept seeks to reduce risk, cost and timescales. More work must therefore be put into getting the base product right, and making it as flexible as possible to allow a steady stream of enhancements over its life. Seiko Epson of Japan are the acknowledged experts at incremental innovation. With only five different varieties of watch movement they currently market over one thousand different models and introduce 100 more every six months.

Process choice

In the previous section the suggestion was introduced that decisions made in the preproduction period have great impact on cost in today's environment. In terms of the level of capital investment to be made initially and sustained, the choice of process – how the product is to be made – is one of these significant factors.

The choice of process is influenced by many factors but the basic trade-offs are clear. Figure 1.5 presents the relationship between product and process evolution. Higher levels of investment may be needed to sustain production in a continuous flow environment, such as chemical production, than in a job shop, for example. Traditionally, the more capital intensive or automated the process, the more constraints exist on a facility's ability to be flexible in the range and degree of complexity of products it can make. The important point is that at any time of product evolution or of process evolution there should be a match between the two; a common point on the diagonal. Problems occur if the type of process does not match the requirement for product.

In the past, the increased automation and efficiency necessary to achieve repetitive manufacture at competitive cost caused an inherently less flexible process. One of the most important features of the new manufacturing environment is the therefore immense contribution made by advanced manufacturing technology (AMT) to shifting the balance of advantage from efficiency towards effectiveness in sustaining competitive advantage. AMT and flexible manufacturing systems (FMS) are targeted towards allowing a manufacturing process to be changed rapidly from producing one product to producing another, or to cope with widely varying or very small batch quantities, whilst retaining the benefit of simulating a continuous flow process.

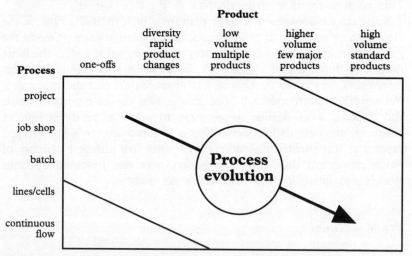

Figure 1.5 Product and process evaluation. Source: Terry Hill (1985), *Manufacturing strategy: The strategic management of the manufacturing function*, Macmillan: London.

Supplier management

With the increased specialisation and focus in manufacturing needed to support a clear and defendable competitive strategy, has come a rise in the importance of the purchasing function. The trend has been for manufacturing entities to lose more and more vertical integration; the result is that they buy in more input material. In some sectors, such as electronics, as much as 90% of direct product cost may be incurred as bought-in components.

Global sourcing in such an environment is essential, with key components being manufactured by perhaps only a handful of major corporations. The value of managing the purchasing aspects of the supply chain and the quality of staff needed to carry out the work are now areas given considerable attention in many companies. With the advent of just-in-time techniques in which single-sourcing and much closer relationships with suppliers are essential, more time and resources are required to identify the right suppliers and monitor the effectiveness of their performance.

Total quality management (TQM)

Perhaps the most significant change in the manufacturing environment of the last few decades has been the focus on quality. Most companies now make reference to quality in their top level strategic objectives. Quality improvement programmes are being started which plan to revolutionise the way companies operate. This section describes some of the background to and the effects of the quality revolution.

At the heart of the TQM concept is a fundamental difference in the approach to bringing about change.[8] The normal way is through step-change – investing capital in advanced technology, new capacity or improved infrastructural support. These are the projects to be found listed in the introduction to the annual bid for capital expenditure authorisation. They probably have a finite life and may succeed in winning a measure of competitive advantage.

An alternative way of improving performance is to tap the ideas and energies of the whole organisation, focusing on incremental enhancements to performance and thereby changing the organisational culture itself. Given a clear vision of where the company is going in the long term, the net effect of many quality programmes may be more productive than the one-off investment strategy alone.

Involving the whole organisation means nothing less than everyone; quality puts people right up front. Recognition of the potential of the individual has raised the profile of many of the traditional activities of the company personnel function. Education and skills training is central to many quality programmes. What is novel about education and training in a quality culture is that it now covers more than the skills needed to perform normal day-to-day work. Whilst acquiring new technology skills for a production engineer or learning how to operate new software for the office clerk are still vital, employees are also trained in problem-solving techniques so they can improve their own activities with less imposition from higher management.

Objectives for quality were formerly confined to product quality and therefore restricted to the shopfloor where products were made. It now embraces every function within the organisation, from purchasing through to marketing and finance.

Quality means:

● Accepting that the only thing that really matters is the customer; if the customer is not happy with the product or service received then, by definition, there is room for improvement. Relating everything to the customers' priorities is ultimately the only way to stay in business.

● Recognising the all-pervasive nature of the customer–supplier relationship. Focusing on **internal** customers and satisfying their needs will also contribute to the final customer's satisfaction. In this way, the computer department supplies the design office engineers with design systems and may agree in advance a level of service which should ensure that these systems are always on-line when required. Figure 1.6 illustrates this concept.

● Moving from inspecting for conformance to a predefined level of quality to preventing the cause of the defect in the first place.

● Instead of an operator making defects which are only recognised 'further down the line' after quality control have done their inspection,

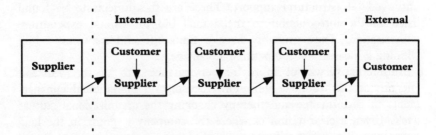

Figure 1.6 Internal and external customers.

making each operator 'personally' responsible for defect-free production in their own domain.

● In production, moving from acceptable quality levels (AQL) to defect levels measured in parts per million. Companies in some industry sectors, like Motorola in electronics, may aspire to attain the elusive 'six-sigma' levels of quality in their production processes: only 3.4 defects per million.

● Zero defect programmes, in which an obsessive drive to produce things right first time is enforced. This is equally applicable to activities as diverse as raising a purchase order or generating the monthly management accounts, as to manufacturing defect-free components in the plant.

● Quality certification programmes such as ISO 9000 (BS 5750). These are based on third-party audits of the extent to which a company can demonstrate that it has complete procedural control over all processes which, if operating properly, will result in the customer receiving the goods on time and to specification.

● Emphasising the total cost of quality as a primary measure of all quality-related activities.

Cost of quality

Quality in some form may account for up to 30% of total costs in manufacturing companies.[9] This cost is not easy to detect and as much as two-thirds of the total cost of quality may be hidden, masquerading as productive work. Typical classifications for quality costs are:

● **Prevention costs**: Costs associated with avoiding machine breakdowns, such as preventive maintenance on production plant. Other prevention costs include quality training, supplier reviews or customer surveys.

● **Appraisal costs**: Costs associated with measuring conformance such as incoming inspection, process control and measuring equipment, set-up inspections before a production batch is started. In the office it would include the heavy cost of managers checking their team's work; answering questions like, 'Do the figures add up?'

● **Internal failure costs**: These are costs incurred as a result of failures in product or internal service which are detected before the delivery to the internal customer. Examples are scrap and rework, in their broadest sense, and loss of value-adding capacity through machine breakdown or failure by an internal company function to meet an agreed service level with its customer department.

• **External failure costs**: These are costs identified with problems occurring after the customer has taken delivery. As well as the most damaging long term cost of lost sales, they cover collection and rework, warranty claims, penalties and liabilities.

Focusing on quality provides a fundamental force for improvement and cost reduction. By realising the full potential of the whole workforce to identify and implement better ways of working, a culture of continual improvement can be generated and, over time, sustained for long term competitive advantage.

Mitsubishi Electric's quality programme in Japan demonstrates the pace of quality-inspired change taking place in some companies today.[10] Fifty thousand employees have spawned over five thousand quality teams and generated upwards of 1.4 million suggestions for improvement every year, winning them bonuses totalling some 400 million yen.

Just-in-time

The philosophy of just-in-time manufacturing became increasingly prominent on the Western industrial scene throughout the 1980s. It is fair to say that it is now widely accepted as being just as effective when applied to companies in the West as in the giants of Japanese manufacturing, its supposed birthplace.[11] Many companies are now endeavouring to use the just-in-time (JIT) concept as a cornerstone of their production and supply chain strategies; the impact both within and between customers and their suppliers has been profound.

The roots of JIT are based on the idea that manufacturing can essentially be regarded as a flow process. The goal is to add value to raw material or components in as short a timescale as possible. In theory, no inventories are then required because input material is received as it is needed and all finished products are immediately sold. Work-in-progress inventories amount only to what is truly being worked on at any time.

No mention of just-in-time would be complete without referring to the classic boating analogy shown in Figure 1.7. The basis of the analogy is that inventory anywhere along the supply chain from materials, work-in-progress (WIP) or finished goods – the water line – is a buffer against problems or lapses in 'right first time quality'; it therefore keeps the orders flowing smoothly through the plant – the boat remains afloat. Cutting production batches in half, for example, can expose the major problems, the rocks, one-by-one as inventory levels fall, providing a readily identifiable series of subjects on which to focus improvement programmes.

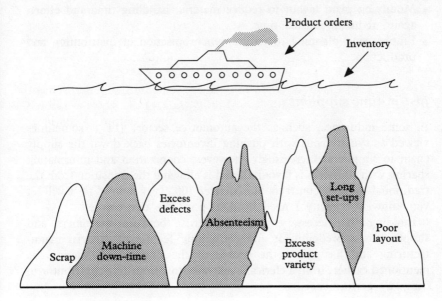

Figure 1.7 JIT boating analogy.

Just-in-time production

'Pull' rather than 'push' scheduling is vital to the effective operation of JIT. Firstly, it is important to appreciate the principle that to avoid holding a finished goods inventory a company must only manufacture products for which it actually has an order. Taken to extremes in the assembly business, no commitment to cost, through purchasing or production, would be made until it is certain that the goods could be immediately sold. Throughout the whole distribution and production process it is therefore possible to envisage a business where all material movement occurs only on demand, with no inventories – customers in effect 'pull' their orders through their suppliers' manufacturing facilities.

To be able to operate in this environment, changes to facilities and priorities must occur:

- Levelling the flow through the manufacturing plant to achieve stability.[12]
- Letting the customer 'dictate' the batch size so that, if necessary, only a single one is made before changing over to a different product. The key to this is reducing, or even eliminating, changeover time (as suggested earlier and made more possible by the many advanced manufacturing technologies reviewed below).

- Modifying plant layout to reduce material handling time and effort; again, reducing wasted time.
- Emphasising planning to ensure synchronisation of distribution and production.

Just-in-time suppliers

In some industries, such as the automotive sector, JIT is sometimes viewed as synonymous with pushing inventories back down the supply chain to suppliers. Increasingly, however, cooperation and information sharing with suppliers is favoured, and is allowing the transition from the traditional supplier contracts like 'deliver 100 every month' to 'I will let you know how many I need by 3.00 p.m. the day before.'

Building the necessary degree of trust between customers and suppliers is a predominant and continuing feature of modern manufacturing and has raised the profile of the purchasing function, as mentioned earlier, from a clerical backwater to a front-line contributor to company performance.

Simultaneous engineering

The increasing importance of 'designing-in' quality through design for manufacturability is a feature of the new manufacturing environment. Many companies now acknowledge the whole area of new product introduction (NPI) as a fertile, and in some sectors untapped, source of competitive opportunity. Like quality, the issue has been discussed for many years but only recently have companies come to realise the enormous benefits to be had from managing the complete design cycle as a discrete and vital process.

In many respects, effective simultaneous engineering – the simultaneous development of the product **and** the manufacturing process – can be regarded as an ideal implementation of both the popular philosophies dealt with in the previous sections: quality and just-in-time.

Reducing 'time-to-market' is not the only objective of focusing on the NPI process – cutting development lead-times can force out the manufacturing issues just as reducing inventories in a just-in-time initiative exposes weaknesses, as shown in the boating analogy. Also, co-locating a new product-focused team of designers and manufacturing people will reduce obstacles to communication and eliminate the design characteristics which may cause defects during manufacture before it is too late.

Another viewpoint which emphasises simultaneous engineering's link with quality is the obligation of designers to take all their customers' points of view; both internally and externally. Understanding the trade-off between designing a product for the final customer's use and designing something that is capable of defect-free manufacture is often overlooked.

Figure 1.8 illustrates the 'over-the-wall' approach to manufacturing, and Figure 1.9 the dynamics of simultaneous engineering in a typical company. The diagrammatic representation of simultaneous engineering in Figure 1.9 is taken from a supplier of automotive components. Here, the cycle-time for new product introduction was reduced from about ten to seven months by replacing the traditional 'over-the-wall' approach, whereby each department worked in isolation, with parallel development of the product and process through cross-functional working.

Codex Corporation of the United States has had spectacular success in a high technology sector where being late-to-market can decimate profits.[13] Implementing rigorous development phase review to force timely decisions, together with robust project management and strict

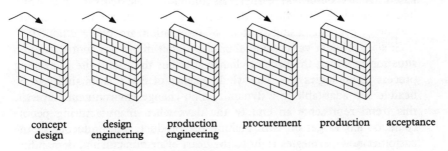

| concept design | design engineering | production engineering | procurement | production | acceptance |

Figure 1.8 'Over-the-wall' manufacturing.

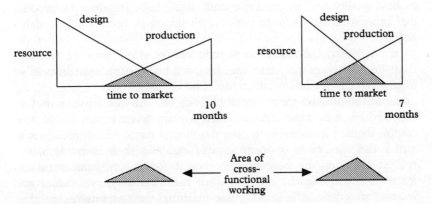

Figure 1.9 Simultaneous engineering.

procedural control, the company achieved reductions of up to 50% in new product introduction projects.

What is important is to take a process perspective on the product development cycle which not only brings designers and manufacturing engineers together early enough but also gives them, like the people in purchasing, a specific and measurable role in contributing to company success.

Advanced manufacturing technology

Across the whole spectrum of the manufacturing process, automation and integration have brought increased productivity from the shopfloor and office. The new manufacturing environment, however, demands that these new process technologies contribute more than just an increase in the speed of unit production – the traditional view of automation – as AMT has a critical role to play in enabling companies to remain competitive in many more ways such as greater flexibility and the time-based factors described earlier. As individual elements of the AMT jigsaw are pieced together with the use of computers and information networks, ever-increasing degrees of integration are being attained.

Greater product variety and shorter product life cycles contribute to a situation in which the pace of change shortens the useful life of existing process technologies too. The whole essence of AMT is its ability to be flexible and adaptable to a dynamic, high change environment. Overall, this trend represents an end to the days when manufacturing people could be left to get on with making the product. The influence of the customer now permeates right to the heart of manufacturing, demanding processes and systems that can respond to short lead-times, make to the highest quality and, at the same time, continually improve the product and process in the battle to preserve shrinking margins – a formidable task.

In the 1970s, the wholesale introduction of AMT into the factory's front-line processes was sometimes regarded by Western companies as an instant remedy for low productivity. The US automotive companies, for example, automated their assembly lines but did not raise output to expected levels because they could not contain defect levels. Insufficient complementary investment in their design and supply chain processes to enable the vehicles to be manufactured easily by their assembly robots robbed them of the benefits they hoped for. Many companies also installed process machinery to reduce manufacturing cycle-times and increase shopfloor 'efficiency'. These machines were expensive, and they had to be kept running to 'pay for themselves'; this led to larger batch quantities which fed through to larger inventories and the classic symptom – a finished goods warehouse full of the wrong products and a backlog of unfulfilled customer orders.

The message here is twofold. Firstly, that the introduction of AMT has to be made in the framework of an overall strategy, one which looks at **all** the elements in the manufacturing and distribution chain to determine the realistic opportunities for benefits from process investment. Secondly, there is the need to focus on investments which reflect the priorities of the customer and reinforce the company's ability to satisfy these. The acquisition of AMT in the context of a more long term perspective compels senior managers to recognise its impact on the whole business of manufacturing as more and more corporate resources are consumed in its acquisition, installation and operation.

The elements of AMT

Having considered the wider aspects of AMT, it is now worth describing the principal elements of it and some of the many acronyms in common usage.

Inter-company communications

The electronic transfer of information between one company and another is known as electronic data interchange (EDI). In many sectors, and increasingly as the JIT philosophy filters through logistics chains, EDI is reducing the time and effort needed to receive and place orders on customers and suppliers. In some industry sectors the use of EDI is becoming an obligation, with customers forcing their suppliers to use their own systems or chosen EDI standards. Although as yet largely confined to invoices and purchase orders (or forward schedules), the use of EDI is expected to explode during the 1990s and to embrace other areas of information exchange including data on prices, quotations, order acknowledgements, order status and even the sharing of complete manufacturing plans to enable suppliers to plan their own programmes accordingly.

Manufacturing planning and control

Material planning and order scheduling in today's manufacturing companies consume a growing quantity of human and technical resources. **Material requirements planning** (MRP) is the process of determining net requirements for raw materials and components after accounting for what is in stock and on order. Versions of MRP are still a fundamental part of even the most highly automated Japanese-style factories; even using just-in-time as a manufacturing principle, advanced commitment to material provisioning is always needed and MRP provides this. **Manufacturing resource planning** (MRPII) goes further by linking medium to long term production plans with existing and planned capacities, and MRP can be extended to enable all factory resource needs to be organised in advance, including machine-time, specialist skills and production space requirements.

With conventional production planning, orders to manufacture are 'launched' or pushed into the manufacturing process using, perhaps, back-scheduling techniques with in-built batch sizes and lead-times. With the spread of automation and more flexible systems, however, there may be many ways to satisfy the same set of customer requirements through using different routes of machines and processes. The ability to simulate the whole production process on a computer is now possible and this allows creation of an optimum production schedule. Scheduling methods, such as the proprietary optimised production technology (OPT) system, may become more widely used. OPT, using a model of all the production processes, can predict and attempt to optimise work scheduling so as to balance the overall flow, minimise the impact of bottlenecks and, ultimately, lead to higher throughput with less inventory.

Design and process planning

The use of computers in design, initially to automate the drafting process in two dimensions and now to model complete structures in three dimensions is one of today's most advanced manufacturing software technologies. Computer automated design (CAD) systems are now able to store and manipulate all the characteristics of a physical object, including its aesthetic qualities, through solid modelling and visualisation, and its physical properties from finite element analysis and stress modelling. Other CAD systems are dedicated to designing specific components, such as printed circuit boards where increased miniaturisation demands ultra-efficient circuit design.

The computerisation of design information provides immense opportunities to employ this data in determining how a product should be built. Metal components are now routinely designed and prototyped on computer-controlled machining centres using computers at every stage. Like design, process planning has, in the past, been viewed as a black art but its impact on quality – through the acknowledged imperative to design for ease of manufacture – is forcing companies to invest in this critical, intermediate process. Expert and knowledge-based systems may have a future role in process planning, thus reducing reliance on key engineers and more effectively integrating designers into the activity.

Manufacturing

The final integration of process planning with factory machinery is enabled through the use of direct numerical control (DNC) or computer numerical control (CNC) tools which can be set in seconds to make different products. The new environment will see greater integration of shopfloor machine tools with production engineering and design.

Assembly automation using robotics will increasingly make a contribution to manufacturing in both high and low volume environments. Currently, however, the flexibility of robots is held back by their relatively underdeveloped 'sight'; they must be instructed to move in a preordained way relative to the work object. Advances in visioning systems, assisted by more powerful computers, will soon enable robots to work more independently, allowing them to operate in less structured and predictable environments.

A key driver to most manufacturing automation is to reduce lost (or wasted) time during the manufacturing process. The use of computers can facilitate this by the reprogramming of process machinery. A recent example of such an application is from Nissan in the United Kingdom. Vehicle body panel welding jigs take a long time to set up because of their varied and complex geometry. Nissan has recently announced a reduction in the time it takes for them to completely re-tool their car body panel jigs from twelve months to three months or less using computerised jig robots in their intelligent body assembly system (IBAS).

Material handling and storage

Automated guided vehicles (AGV) linked to automated storage and retrieval systems (ASRS) are now common features in many plants. These systems, which are linked with material planning and order scheduling, are able to work round the clock on such tasks as putting together kits of components ready for assembly or keeping automatic machines fed with the right parts in the right order. Higher stacking heights in the warehouse mean less floor space is needed which in turn reduces material handling time. The advent of more 'lean' production methods with their lower inventory levels throughout the whole system, has embarrassed some companies who, having invested heavily in ASRS, have found that they are now seriously underused.

Flexible manufacturing and group technology

The essence of a flexible manufacturing system (FMS) is the bringing together of a combination of a carefully chosen collection of machine tools, robots and material handling mechanisms under the control of a computer which coordinates each device simultaneously to synchronise workflow.[14] The FMS is configured in such a way as to allow the whole system to manufacture a family of products or parts. Integral with the continuous production cycle, a typical FMS should also include the capability to monitor 'quality' – in the form of finished part dimensions – dynamically updating tool positioning to maintain parts within predefined tolerances. In this way, the true capabilities of numerically controlled process machinery can be exploited, with single unit batches, instant set-up and minimal work-in-progress inventory.

Group technology (GT) is a method of classification which allows products to be analysed in such a way as to identify similar design and processing characteristics. Using this information, processes are grouped together to reduce material handling and to benefit from the inherent advantages of being able to manage like processes together. Such manufacturing cells within plants which formerly had traditional, functionally organised shop layouts – in which process machines were grouped purely by type – pose a challenge to existing company infrastructures. For this reason many companies have chosen to move to GT-based cells gradually, setting them up for a part of their products or processes, to monitor their success and learn from their experiences.

Standards and advanced technology

Despite the opportunities for more effective manufacturing through carefully targeted AMT, an issue has emerged during AMT's development over recent years that has a fundamental effect on the success of its application. From one perspective, standards are of prime importance in exploiting AMT, but from another, standards in terms of how things are done in the workplace may, in many cases, constrain innovation and inhibit the process of continual improvement.

It will be clear that in many situations AMT only becomes really useful when computers are used to integrate related processes – linking islands of automation together in what is popularly regarded as manufacturing's Holy Grail – computer integrated manufacturing (CIM). Although commentators have cast doubt on attaining CIM as a worthy end in itself, the problems still exist on a smaller scale. The wide variety of different types of hardware and software, and the difficulties encountered in passing information between them have resulted in the need for common technical standards. The development of agreed data network communication protocols and data formats to overcome these problems will be an increasingly important issue in manufacturing.

In some sectors, the lack of standards may impede progress towards fully exploiting some of the benefits of AMT. Furthermore, there will be increasing pressure to conform or risk destructive 'information isolation' in which a company finds itself unable to keep up with the pace of information flow, both internally and, worse still, with its customers and suppliers.

The future

The pace of change in manufacturing techniques and philosophies shows no sign of abating, and the developments described in this chapter form only a snapshot of current thinking at a point in time. The only certainty is that competing with world-class businesses will require the relentless pursuit of continuous improvement in every aspect of the business and this includes the development of world-class approaches to performance measurement and cost management. The following chapters describe such developments to date.

References

1 J. Stanley (1990), Globalisation strategy and regional management against a framework of block economies, Global Conference on Management Innovation, Tokyo; CMI Conference Proceedings

2 K. Iwaki (1990), A framework for growth: Sony's case, Global Conference on Management Innovation, Tokyo; CMI Conference Proceedings

3 T. Susuki (1990), Globalisation of management and human resources development, Global Conference on Management Innovation, Tokyo; CMI Conference Proceedings

4 M.E. Porter (1985), *Competitive Advantage: Creating and Sustaining Superior Performance*, Free Press: New York

5 T. Hill (1985), *Manufacturing Strategy: The Strategic Management of the Manufacturing Function*, Macmillan: London

6 C.J.S. Bentley (1991), Manufacturing strategies for the 1990s: a framework for innovative decision-making, *European Business Journal*, vol. 3, no. 2, pp. 31–8.

7 H. Mather (1988), *Competitive Manufacturing*, Prentice Hall: Englewood Cliffs, NJ

8 D. Kynaston (1990), Company-wide quality improvement, Manufacturing Strategies for the '90s, Birmingham; KPMG Peat Marwick/ Financial Times International Conference Proceedings, Birmingham

9 J. Atkinson (1990), *Increasing Profitability by Managing the Total Cost of Quality*, KPMG Peat Marwick: Chicago, IL

10 T. Ito (1990), Transition in Mitsubishi Electric's TQC program, Global Conference on Management Innovation, Tokyo; CMI Conference Proceedings

11 G.C. Stevens (1988), Can JIT work in the UK?, *Logistics Today*, vol. 7, no. 1, pp. 6–9.

12 S. Uchikawa (1990), The Toyota production system today: current issues in just-in-time, Global Conference on Management Innovation, Tokyo; CMI Conference Proceedings

13 R. Schroeder (1989), Improving quality and reducing cycle-time in new product development: a case study, Integrated Design and Manufacturing Strategies for Business Transformation, KPMG Peat Marwick International Conference on Manufacturing Renaissance; IFS Conference Proceedings, London

14 P.W. Moir (1989), *Efficient Beyond Imagining: CIM and its Applications for Today's Industry*, Ellis Horwood Limited: Chichester

CHAPTER 2

Information requirements

Chapter 1 has described the extent of the changes to the manufacturing sector in the last 30 years. This chapter follows the effect these changes have had on the cost structure of manufacturing business, the resulting decline in usefulness of traditional approaches to cost management and performance measurement, and how, from a number of sources, there have been new developments to meet new information needs.

Changing cost structures

The starting point for this chapter is to consider how the typical cost profile of a manufacturing business has changed over the last 30 years as represented in Figure 2.1. The proportion of cost that is made up by direct labour has shrunk dramatically and is now thought to average about 15% in the United Kingdom. In many high technology industries the proportion has shrunk to even less, and in a 'lights out' factory (fully

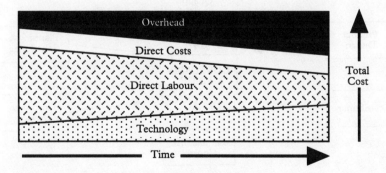

Figure 2.1 The change in the typical cost profile of a manufacturing business over the last 30 years.

automated so that the lights can be turned out) there is no direct labour at all. The cost which was direct labour has now been taken up by a greater proportion of indirect costs (overheads) including the increased cost of technology, whether information technology or automation on the factory floor. The reasons for this shift in costs do not require much explanation. A plant tour around a factory in the 1960s compared to a similar factory in the 1990s would reveal just how few people are needed on direct operations because of the effects of technology, automation and manufacturing methods, as described in Chapter 1. It is assumed, for these purposes, that direct costs such as raw materials have remained constant, but this will of course depend on the specifics of the industry.

This change in cost structure has a greater significance, however, than merely shifting budgets from one expense category to another. The real significance is in the shift from where the essence of value is created in the business. The trend has been to move away from the idea that value is created in the actual shopfloor manufacturing process where conversion or assembly takes place. This is no longer necessarily the case for most manufacturing businesses. The activities in overhead areas have become an important basis of adding value and often where competitive advantage is created. Figure 2.2 represents this.

Thus, being effective on the shopfloor alone is not enough. It is through better design, production scheduling, customer service, etc., that the business is able to outperform its competitors, as well as having reached the same level of efficiency on the factory floor. Indeed, many businesses have called into question what their business really is. As a well-known example, many players in the automotive and aerospace industries have decided that the essence of the business is in the ability to design and assemble. Manufacturing is limited to only those

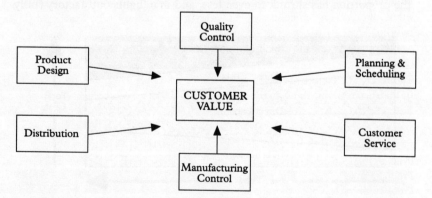

Figure 2.2 Overhead areas are important for adding value to a product.

components of key importance where it is essential to retain key competencies; other manufacturing is subcontracted. Here the business has recognised what it is good at and what other businesses can do better. The simple machining or pressing of components is not something which an automotive or aerospace business has to be geared up to do very well if it can use a subcontractor that can perform the activity much more effectively (and some machine shop businesses are totally geared up to do just this). Whilst it would be inappropriate in this book to explore further the identification of core competencies[1] and the basis of creating competitive advantage, it is clear that overhead areas can no longer be regarded just as cost burdens. The activities in overhead areas require to be managed just as effectively as those on the factory floor in a performance measurement and cost management system.

The final point to emphasise regarding the change in the nature of overheads can be made by comparing the factors of competition of most industries between the 1960s and 1990s as summarised in Table 2.1. The need to remain competitive in the face of all these factors typically leads to greater complexity in the business and it is business **complexity** which typically drives up indirect cost. It is this phenomenon which led Wickham Skinner, one of the fathers of manufacturing strategy, to observe: 'the focused factory will always outproduce, undersell and quickly gain advantage over the complex factory.'[2] Thus, in simple terms, a factory producing a limited product range to a few customers will have much lower overheads than a factory producing similar products but in a very wide range and to many customers.

The challenge for management is to understand the optimum level of complexity which balances the advantages of the focused factory (or focused units within a factory) with the needs of the marketplace and a coherent commercial strategy. A meaningful approach to cost management and performance measurement on the factory floor **and** in the overhead areas is a prerequisite to being able to strike this balance.

Despite the great changes to manufacturing businesses described

Table 2.1 The factors of competition for most industries from the 1960s to the 1990s.

	1960s → → → → → 1990s
Product functionality	increasing ⎯⎯⎯⎯⎯→
Product range	increasing ⎯⎯⎯⎯⎯→
Product life cycles	shortening ←⎯⎯⎯⎯
Defect rates	reducing ←⎯⎯⎯⎯
Delivery time	reducing ←⎯⎯⎯⎯

earlier, the resulting change to cost structures and the changes in market demands, it is arguable that fundamental advances have not been made in developments for cost management and performance measurement. As a result, in many organisations, a lot of management information has become irrelevant and even discredited and the opportunity to move the business forward at its full potential has been lost. The main elements of traditional approaches to cost management and performance measurement are considered below.

Standard costing and overhead recovery

The essential feature of standard costing is the inclusion of raw material and direct labour usage at predetermined prices, monitored against actuals to produce financial variances. Variances are attributed as being due to efficiency, volume or price and the intention is that they are used to control factory operations. The product costs from a standard costing are typically used for stock valuation and cost of sales purposes, and sometimes for decision support regarding setting selling prices, make versus buy, etc. This emphasis on financial variances and cost of sales has been one of the attractions of standard costing for many accountants, because it provides such strong support for the period profit and loss account and balance sheet.

The disadvantages of standard costing are now, however, becoming increasingly recognised:

● The building up of standard costs implies that achieving a zero variance for, say, waste or efficiency, is acceptable. This is in contradiction to continuous improvement programmes where the emphasis is on always striving to achieve better performance. While supporters of standard costing argue that demanding targets can be regularly updated in standard costs, this will not usually be as effective as simple and clear measures which focus **directly on** the performance issues in question and show the trend over time towards a target.

● The feedback time in standard cost systems for operational control purposes is usually quite long because of the time required to identify the variance and trace it back to source (which is often tied to the monthly accounts cycle). The essence of operational control should be that information is immediate so that anything wrong can be put right without further loss. Furthermore, a standard costing system converts operating data into financial information which only has to be converted back again to operating data before it can be of real use to operating management.

Most standard costing systems also incorporate overhead recovery. Thus, not only are direct labour and raw material and component costs included, but an element, or all, of factory costs and overheads. The usual method for doing this is through volume-related allocations and burden rates such as percentage additions to material cost, direct labour overhead burden rates and machine-time overhead burdens. The principle of variances is therefore extended to the overhead areas with resulting price and volume variances.

There are very real problems associated with this overhead recovery model of the business:

• The link between the overhead allocation and the product is largely arbitrary and reflects neither the real demand for resources that each product places on the business nor how overhead costs will behave if volumes increase or decrease. This point is returned to in Chapter 4 'Product costing'.

• It encourages overproduction, as the recovery of overheads in the product costs ends up in period end stock values, increasing period profit. (Although this is merely an accounting timing difference as the closing stock in one period forms the opening stock in the next, it is, however, an all too frequently used device.) It is therefore at variance with just-in-time principles.

• It encourages production of the easy-to-make items, which can be pushed through to recover overheads producing a positive variance, rather than the more difficult to make products. This is at variance with schedule adherence performance measures and MRP philosophies.

Again, one of the reasons that this type of overhead recovery has been so popular with accountants is that it supports the explanation of period profit and loss accounts.

Purchase price variance (PPV) has long been an important performance measure in many businesses. It is often derived from standard costing systems. While PPV clearly has some value as a measure, the risks of overemphasising it are:

• Price is only one measure of a supplier's performance. Defect rates, quality, delivery frequency, on-time delivery, reliability and new product frequency lead-times are also important and can have a greater effect on the business than a slightly cheaper price. Ideally, the **total** impact of competing suppliers on the business should be assessed, which would include all the factors listed above.

● It can lead to bulk buying to obtain quantity discounts, resulting in overstocking and possible obsolescence.

Financial budgeting

Budgeting is, arguably, one of the most important parts of the management process as it is the time when decisions should be made about the outlook for the coming year, what level of resources will be required, how they should be utilised around the business and what the expected result for the year should be. Instead, many budgets are little more than financial forecasts engineered to suit the needs of head office, and within these, overhead budgets are built up from the current or previous year's spend, adjusted for new projects and inflation. This subject is returned to in Chapter 6 'Budgeting and cost reporting'. The essential point for now is that the purpose of many budgets is mainly to support the forecast profit and loss account for the coming period, rather than really understanding how resources can be most effectively employed in the business.

Monthly management accounts

The monthly management accounts are treated as being of central importance to many businesses and many operating decisions are made by managers with direct reference to the effect on them. They form the link between the annual financial accounts and the subsidiary systems, as shown in Figure 2.3.

The preparation and interpretation of the monthly accounts and the systems to support them, along with the reforecasting which tends to go on as well, are often major consumers of time and resource in the accounts department and elsewhere. Yet few organisations question whether all this effort represents value for money and whether an extensive focus on monthly management accounts is appropriate for a modern manufacturing business. Later chapters in this book will examine how some of the time and resource currently given to financial reporting might be better spent on managing costs and understanding performance.

The impact of financial reporting

The common theme of all the traditional approaches described here is that they strongly relate to, or are part of, **financial** reporting, in the

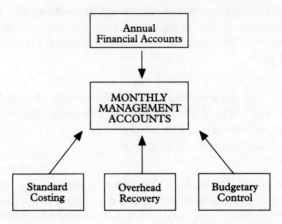

Figure 2.3 Monthly management accounts link subsidiary systems
to the annual financial accounts.

form of period profit and loss accounts and balance sheets. It is
appropriate at this point then to refer to another book which expands
greatly on this point and has had, arguably, more effect on management
accounting than any other in recent decades. *Relevance Lost: The Rise
and Fall of Management Accounting*[3] by H. Thomas Johnson and Robert
S. Kaplan was first published in 1987, and can be described as the
history of management accounting. It traces the development of
management accounting techniques through the nineteenth and the first
half of the twentieth century, with the emphasis always on providing
information which was relevant to the decisions being taken at the time.
Thus, return on capital employed was developed in response to the
creation of 'divisions' within businesses as a way of monitoring their
performances. Similarly, direct labour overhead burden rates were
developed (at a time when direct labour was by far the dominant cost) in
response to growing product diversity and the need to cost each product
type.

The book then traces over the last 30 years or so the growth in interest
of financial reporting (that is, financial statements reported to the outside
world). Thus, at a time when a great deal of effort has gone into:

- the emergence of accounting standards, which seek to achieve greater
  consistency and benefits from financial reporting;
- the research and development of techniques which seek to explain the
  relationship between financial results, share prices and risk; and
- financial engineering, including off-balance sheet engineering and the
  treatment of subsidiaries and acquired companies;

Relevance Lost argues that **management accounting** did not adapt to remain relevant to the great changes in the manufacturing industry because of its subservience to the needs of financial reporting. To quote from the book:

> Today's management accounting information, driven by the procedures and cycle of the organisation's financial reporting system, is too late, too aggregated and too distorted to be relevant for managers' planning and control decisions. (p. 1.)

The most graphic example of this which is explained in *Relevance Lost* concerns the treatment of overheads in product costs. Because of the increase in indirect costs and overheads, described earlier, set against falling direct labour costs, many direct labour overhead burden rates have reached proportions of 1000% or more. Clearly such a burden rate is only good for putting overheads onto products *en bloc*, so that in aggregate there is a precisely traceable overhead recovery in stock values and cost of sales. These are financial reporting requirements, as the only reason to value stock is to calculate period profit. Product costs based on 1000% direct labour overhead burden rates cannot hope to reflect the real overhead resource demands that individual products place on the business. Yet such individual product costs are frequently being calculated and sometimes used for decision-making as if they were still relevant. Thus, product costing became subservient to the needs of financial reporting rather than providing useful management accounting information.

Although *Relevance Lost* has been widely acclaimed for the impact it has had, critics argued that it failed to put anything concrete in the place of the approaches to cost management being criticised. Meanwhile, the book went on to become something of a bestseller, especially in the United States. It is sometimes said, cynically, that the book was not being bought by accountants but by chief executive officers who wanted to read what they knew all along, that their chief financial officers had got it wrong.

New approaches

The consistent trend that has emerged concerning the new approaches to performance measurement and cost management has been to move away from supporting the accounting model of the business to approaches which reflect the reality of what is happening and service the needs of managers for decision-making. This inevitably means:

- less emphasis on financial numbers;
- concern with being approximately right, rather than being precise but unhelpful;
- providing information at intervals when it is needed, to suit decision-making, rather than being driven by a monthly reporting cycle;
- looking forwards, with an emphasis on decision-making and action, rather than looking backwards at historical analysis; and
- looking outside the business, as well as inside.

The **structure** of the approaches also reflects how businesses work. It is always dangerous to put forward generic models of businesses but the simple framework shown in Figure 2.4 often makes sense.

The essential point is that strategy is formulated (formally or informally) taking account of market opportunities and conditions, the behaviour of competitors and the availability of technology. The important point here, however, is that the typical outcome of strategy development is an understanding of what products and customers the business will pursue. This should include, of course, thinking through

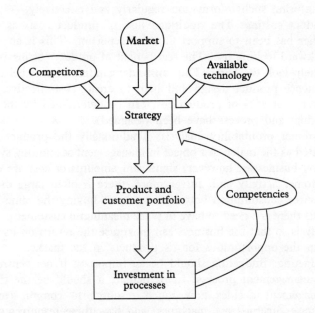

Figure 2.4 How businesses work.

the nature of the business's competitive advantage and how to meet the customer's criteria for placing orders. The business is then in a position to know what **processes** it needs in order to be able to sell and deliver the products to its customers. These processes will be those on the shopfloor, the physical manufacturing process, and the indirect processes which, as described earlier, are increasingly important in creating customer value. It is typically the creation and maintenance of these **processes** which determine the cost level in a business. The final point relating to the business model is to acknowledge that the determination of strategy is fundamentally affected by what the business is good at doing, hence the competency line feeding back up into the strategy box in Figure 2.4.

Using this simple model it is now possible to consider the new approaches to performance measurement and cost management information requirements:

- External information for strategic management: Given that strategy is largely formulated by reference to competitors, the market and the availability of new technology, it is important to monitor regularly trends, events and movements relating to these factors. This will help track progress, assess the need to reposition and to make tactical changes. Research[4] suggests that many companies are poor at monitoring such information regularly and effectively.

- Product costing: The traditional use of product costs as described earlier has been to support financial reporting. This is an essentially backward-looking use. The real benefit of product costing is to use it to help look **forwards**. Thus an understanding of cost behaviour can influence product design and help to create cost-effective processes (given that 85% of product cost can be determined by the time the product and process have been designed).

- Customer profitability analysis: Traditionally the product has been treated as the major cost object in management accounting systems. In many businesses, however, significant amounts of cost are driven by customer activity and, furthermore, there is often large diversity of resource consumption between customers buying the same products. Thus there is a need to have in place meaningful customer profitability analysis so that the business can maximise the return on its resources from the opportunities for its products in the market.

- Budgeting: Budgeting should be an important if not central part of the management process. In particular, it should be the time when management decides how much resource to commit (to people, premises, technology, machines) and how these resources should be employed, given the prospects for the business and its strategic intent regarding its product and customer portfolio. Effective budgeting, therefore, is concerned with allocating the appropriate level of resource to put the necessary processes in place to meet these needs.

- Operational control: Given the size and complexity of modern businesses, it is important to have in place a system that gives fast and effective feedback to management that operations are carrying on according to plan and in particular that **action** is being taken to solve problems and meet output targets.

- Performance measurement: The goal of every business is to maximise its value and this is measured in financial terms. Merely measuring the financial performance of the business will not, however, enable managers to know what they need to do to **achieve** the financial results. Furthermore, the performance measures chosen are the visible manifestation of what is important to the business if it is to meet its goals. They are the factors that will affect managers' **behaviour** and, if properly used, are a key tool in implementing strategy within the business. Thus, a system of performance measures is needed which guides managers towards doing the right things (affecting their behaviour) and gives them goals and targets to aim for. Typically a balanced set of performance measures will include the key factors to get right in the business process, from the customer's point of view and the factors that mean the organisation itself is growing, learning and developing. The performance measures used should clearly link directly to the strategy for the business (how it achieves competitive advantage and adds value) and from this what the priorities are for the business if it is to achieve its objectives.

- Process improvement: Given the importance of processes to nearly all businesses, as they are the main users of resource and the means by which value is delivered to customers, it is appropriate to have in place a mechanism to achieve regular process improvements. Thus, whilst operational controls and performance measures will indicate how well the business is doing what it decided to do, process improvement techniques will question and reassess how processes could be carried out more effectively to reduce cost, enhance timeliness and service, increase flexibility and improve quality.

The divisions used above are, to an extent, artificial in that they cannot be separated from each other and should form part of a consistent and coherent total approach. Furthermore, the individual circumstances of businesses and industries will mean that not all the approaches will always be needed. Nevertheless, the headings provide a reasonable model of the performance measurement and cost management information needs of managers which reflects the way decisions have to be made.

These headings are therefore also used as a structure for later chapters of this book.

References

1 G. Hamel and C.K. Prahalad (1990), The Core Competence of the Corporation, *Harvard Business Review*, vol. 68, no. 3, pp. 79–91
2 W. Skinner (1974), The Focused Factory, *Harvard Business Review*, vol. 52, no. 3
3 H.T. Johnson and R.S. Kaplan (1987), *Relevance Lost: The Rise and Fall of Management Accounting*, Harvard Business School Press: Boston, MA
4 The Harris Research Centre (1990), *Information for Strategic Management: A Study of Leading Companies*, Manchester

CHAPTER 3

Activity-based approaches

Chapter 2 described the increasingly wide and flexible approach now being taken to performance measurement and cost management, and why this is needed to reflect the reality of decision-making in a business. Although activity-based techniques have usually gone under the label of activity-based costing (ABC), which is often associated with the narrow use of product costing, it is now clear that an activity basis is useful, if not essential, in many aspects of understanding cost behaviour. This chapter gives an overview of the rapid development of activity-based techniques to support new approaches to cost management and it provides a common understanding for the chapters which follow.

Even before *Relevance Lost* was published there had been increasing interest in approaches to costing which considered activities to be a building block for understanding product costs and other aspects of cost management. These had not all gone under the label of ABC and, arguably, some costing systems developed decades ago had achieved similar results. Nevertheless, from the mid-1980s onwards, the interest in activity-based techniques developed dramatically. This interest grew from several often connected sources, and which occurred first and which was the most important need not be of concern. The two main sources will be discussed here.

The first of these is Robert Kaplan himself, working mostly with a fellow Harvard professor, Robin Cooper. Between them, Cooper and Kaplan developed a series of case studies and articles which form the basis of much of the thinking on the subject that goes under the label of ABC. Their interest, in particular, started with the use of activity costs as a means of building up product costs, as an alternative to large direct labour overhead burden rates and other arbitrary means of overhead apportionment. From this they developed into customer profitability and other uses of the techniques. Thus Kaplan was able to answer the critics of *Relevance Lost* by pointing to the hard evidence of his and Cooper's case studies as a better way of costing. Cooper and Kaplan's articles and case studies are too numerous to mention here but the most significant have been published in one volume, *The Design of Cost Management Systems*.[1] These articles and case studies are interesting in that they show, over a period, how Cooper and Kaplan's thinking developed at each stage to complete the conceptual circle of how activity-based costs can be used to model cost behaviour and, of equal importance, how the major practical aspects of implementation and use can be handled.

The second source mentioned here in the development of activity-based techniques is CAM-I (Computer Aided Manufacturing International), a not-for-profit research cooperative sponsored by leading American and European industrial companies, management consultancies and academics. CAM-I is made up of a number of programmes, all of which were originally concerned with manufacturing and engineering approaches and techniques, with the emphasis being on making rapid advances in manufacturing effectiveness, just as the Japanese had done so successfully. By 1986, it was realised within CAM-I that to support the developments in manufacturing a new approach to cost management was required, and a cost management system (CMS) programme was launched. Interestingly, this CMS programme has become by far the most successful of all those run by CAM-I, reflecting perhaps the latent dissatisfaction which many organisations felt with their traditional approaches.

It was decided very early on within the CMS programme to adopt an activity-based technique in the development of an approach to cost management, and this led to another book: *Cost Management for Today's Advanced Manufacturing: The CAM-I Conceptual Design*.[2] The book, as the title states, is conceptual in nature and was to be the first of three phases of the CMS programme, to be followed by a systems design phase and then implementation at a number of sites as prototypes. However, it is the output from this first phase which has had the most impact. The CMS approach regards activity costs as a 'building block' for a cost management system that meets, or at least contributes to, all cost management needs.

Both Cooper and Kaplan's approach and that developed within CMS are based on an analysis of activities as a basis of understanding how resources are used in a business. The difference between the two is largely one of emphasis, with Cooper and Kaplan focusing more on product costs while the CMS approach considers product costing to be of only equal importance to other cost management needs. These two points of emphasis are merging with time and experience.

In the United Kingdom there has been tremendous interest in activity-based approaches in the late 1980s and early 1990s. At first, the impetus for this was mainly provided by management consultancies such as KPMG Management Consulting, with extra interest provided by articles, speakers and case studies crossing the Atlantic. The initial response to ABC from UK academics ranged mostly from cold to lukewarm with few adding to the debate (although there are some worthy exceptions to this). The main response from the management accounting establishment, in the form of The Chartered Institute of Management Accountants, was to publish a booklet *Management Accounting: Evolution Not Revolution*[3] in 1988. This booklet was partly in response to the feeling that exaggerated claims were being made about the benefits of ABC. It concluded that traditional approaches to cost management were adequate if properly applied and that the case for ABC had yet to be proven. This was a fairly consistent theme from academics in the United Kingdom, and only in the early 1990s, as more and more UK case studies published show the benefits to be obtained, is it becoming accepted by UK academics as a valid technique.

While, perhaps, sceptical academics in the United Kingdom have formed a valuable service in questioning activity-based approaches, thus helping to clarify thinking on the subject, a lot of the criticism it has attracted has been from those who saw it only as the rearrangement of historic overhead costs on products. It is true that some early ABC case studies did feature this aspect of the technique, but it is not difficult given the will and even a little imagination to see beyond this quickly and to realise the wider use of activity costs to manage the business.

The continuing interest in activity-based approaches, reflected in the number of articles, conferences and training courses on the subject, and most importantly the number of implementations, is testimony in itself to the dissatisfaction many organisations have with their traditional approaches, and there is little doubt that activity-based approaches will become an integral part of management accounting, although in a more mature manner than was at first the case.

Principles of activity-based approaches

To start at the beginning, it is worth a reminder that the ultimate measure of success for any business is to generate and sustain an inflow of cash which is greater than the outflow. The essence of business management is to buy resources (causing a cash outflow) and put them in place so as to make or provide something for which other people will pay, and which has a greater resulting cash inflow (revenue or capital value). Anything that accountants do to model the business in terms of period profit and loss accounts and balance sheets is, arguably, ultimately subservient to this (although in some organisations it would sometimes appear to be the other way around).

The central issue in cost management is how to decide how much resource to put in place in each area of the business, how to use it effectively and then to measure performance in achieving objectives. The focus of most traditional cost reporting is on the resources bought. Thus, cost reports typically show wages, salaries, rent, etc., by department in accordance with the organisational hierarchy (see Figure 3.1). This is fine as far as it goes, but shows nothing about how those resources are being used by the manager in charge of them, other than what is known generally about what goes on in that department. If we take an example such as a production planning department, traditional cost reporting might show exactly how much has been spent in the month, year-to-date, against budget and last year, by line item, down to the nearest pound, after going to a lot of trouble to match costs to time periods through accounting techniques such as depreciation and accruals. It does not, however, give any clue as to:

- What takes up the time of production planning staff
- Whether the right amount of resource is in place
- What factors cause them to have to do what they do so often
- How different products, customers and suppliers influence these factors
- Whether it is costing less or more than it should to do the things they do
- How to go about doing things more effectively

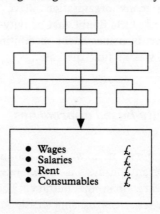

Figure 3.1 Traditional vertical view of costs.

An activity-based approach attempts to answer some of these questions or at least to give information to help ask the right questions. This is because an activity-based approach is based on the premise that, in order to understand how resources are being used, it is necessary to understand the activities being performed. Thus, it is activities that consume resources; this is shown in Figure 3.2. Understanding what activities are performed, and costing them, gives **visibility** as to how resources are being used, providing a better basis for managing them.

What might these activities be? It is important to understand that there are no predetermined lists. Although the activities in, for example, the production planning department may be similar in many organisations, the only way really to find out is to carry out activity analysis. This is mainly done by asking the people who work there. There is no alternative to asking and observing; activity analysis cannot be carried out any other way. Thus the definition of activities has to follow the circumstances of the organisation in question and the use to which the information will be put. The level of detail of activity analysis will vary too, depending on the use to which it is being put. Activities are typically defined somewhere between tasks and functions (see Figure 3.3). Work measurement, with all the detail that that involves, is usually at the task level, whereas traditional cost reporting is usually at the functional level. Activity analysis is usually in between these two, such that the volume of information is manageable yet sufficiently detailed to be useful.

From this simple example it is possible to imagine how activity analysis could be undertaken in every department or section in a

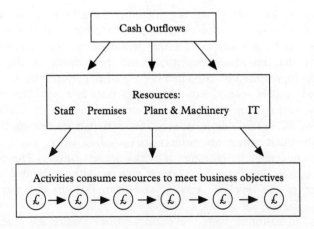

Figure 3.2 An activity-based approach is based on an understanding of how activities use resources.

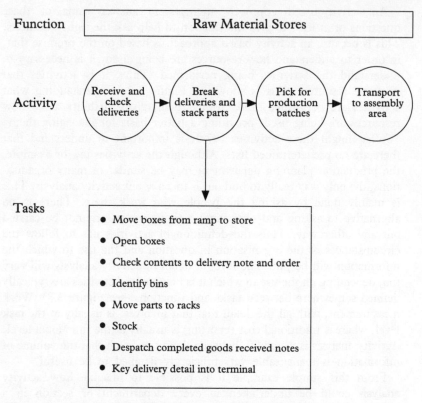

Figure 3.3 Activities are defined between tasks and functions.

business, by looking at each one, defining the activities, and allocating the relevant costs to activities on appropriate bases. If this were done there would be a snapshot, for the period of the time chosen, of the activities that had been performed and how much of the business resource (represented by cost) had been used to perform them. (It can be imagined, and is soon discovered in practice, how well the technique suits the various functions that make up the business. It works best in functions where fairly discrete, repetitive activities take place. Functions and individuals which are project-orientated or where there are large numbers of constantly changing activities are less suited.) The next stage is to think about how the cost of each activity is divided by some indicator of the **level** of activity, and from this the cost per unit of activity. Figure 3.4 shows a framework for this.

Thus, to continue with the example from Figure 3.3, the activity 'break deliveries and stack parts' might use up three man years of effort per annum, which with related costs comes to £50,000 per year, and

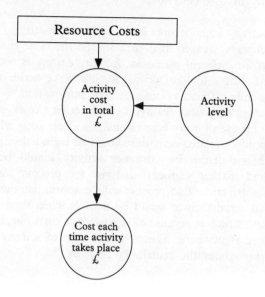

Figure 3.4 Indicating the level of activity.

takes place about 4,000 times, costing an average £12.50 per delivery. Such an analysis, even at this stage, can give a useful insight to management about how resources are being used and prompt questions about effectiveness and value for money.

Having created activity costs, both in total and for each time the activity takes place, it is now possible to start to arrange them in different ways to help understand cost behaviour and resource use. To do this, it is necessary to think what the **cost objects** should be. This part of the process is as important as the activity analysis itself, and is where, frequently, activity-based exercises go wrong.

Early cases of studies using ABC often treated products as the sole cost object, such that **all** costs were allocated on some sort of activity basis to create fully absorbed product costs. While this approach has a neatness to it and at first sight may be attractive, the reality is that in most businesses large amounts of indirect cost simply do not behave as a function of product volume. Thus to create fully absorbed product costs requires arbitrary cost allocations which do not reflect the reality of how costs behave and is only one way of looking at activity costs.

Instead, the key to understanding cost behaviour through activity analysis is to consider:

- What the information will be used for
- The reality of cost behaviour

Thus, the activity costs become building blocks which can be stacked in a number of ways, as seen in Figure 3.5. So the same base information can be used for different purposes. Activity costing is not therefore an end in itself, but a tool or technique to achieve better results in the provision of many forms of management information.

Furthermore, to reflect reality, not all activity costs will always be appropriate for use in every type of analysis. Thus costs which are being driven by product-related activities should be included in product costs; costs which are driven by customer activity should be included in customer and market segment analysis; for process costing, all the activity costs driven by that process will be appropriate; and so on. The only time all activity costs would be used is when they are shown by responsibility, which is because all a business's costs normally fall into a budget centre somewhere. These various uses of activity costs will be described throughout the remaining chapters.

Costs to include

The next question to ask is what categories of costs should be included in activity costs. There are two views here. The view put forward in *Cost*

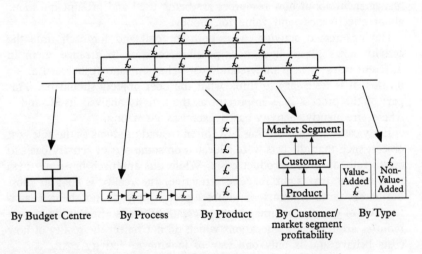

Figure 3.5 Activity costs are building blocks for many forms of management information.

Management for Today's Advanced Manufacturing is that **all traceable costs** should be included to create **fully absorbed** activity costs. This would therefore include space costs, depreciation of machines, and costs from other cost centres. This is attractive conceptually, in that **all** resource consumption is taken into account in the activity cost and, so the argument goes, all resources are therefore managed at the activity level. In practice, fully absorbed activity costs can become very complex and create a hierarchy of cross-charging which confuses the understanding of cost behaviour. The alternative view is that the costs included in an activity cost should be those relevant to the decision being made, to create **decision-relevant information**. Thus, for example, activity costs in the personnel department should not include office space costs if space is outside the control of the personnel manager, and the activity costs are being used on this occasion to help set and monitor the personnel manager's budget. Space costs would then be managed on another basis which might not be activity-based. A good rule is to strike a balance between excessive system complexity and an approach that suits the circumstances, information needs and requirements of the organisation.

The second part of the answer to the question of what costs to include in activity costs is to consider what is meant by cost. In the context of cost management it is necessary to differentiate between two aspects of cost. The first is **spending**, and the second is **resource consumption**. This was shown earlier, in Figure 3.2, where cash outflows provide resources and activities consume those resources. The important point, however, is that changes in the **level of activity** rarely mean an automatic change in the **amount of resource** provided and in turn the spending level (see Figure 3.6). So, typically, a level of resource has to be put in place to cope with the highest level of activity. If the activity level falls, there is unused resource. If the activity level increases, actions such as overtime, rescheduling, postponement of non-essential activities can occur, but if persistent enough then a more permanent increase in resource provision has to take place.

It is also necessary to consider the links between resource provision and **spending**. Not all forms of resource provision result in the same spending changes. The simple model in Figure 3.7 shows both these points. As the activity level increases there will be a direct increase in the resources consumed. For example, every sales order requires an average two hours of clerical labour and one hour of computer time to process. But the number of sales orders will fluctuate each day. If no orders are received, the spending on resources continues but it is unused resource. When, however, the activity level increases significantly a new sales order processing clerk has to be taken on. Thus the spending and resource provision will increase in steps. Other forms of resource

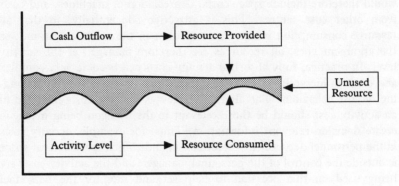

Figure 3.6 The link between resources provided and resources consumed.

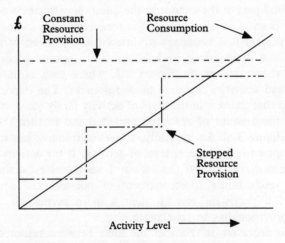

Figure 3.7 The change in spending with activity level.

provision and the associated spending, such as rent and rates for space, are constant unless the building is either closed down or extended. Finally, some resources, such as fixed assets, require one-off spending when purchased and the resource is in place until it wears out. It is important to realise then, that activity-based approaches consider the **cost of resources consumed**. This is a starting point for also considering how **spending** might change, but the two are not the same.

When activity levels fall and there is significant excess resource in place, it is important to highlight this factor. For example, if a process costing £5m a year is set up to manufacture a product within an anticipated volume of 50,000 a year, the indirect cost would be £100 per unit. If the volume falls to 40,000 per year, it is often the case that not much of the cost will change (reinforcing the point made earlier). If the cost of the process reduces to £4.8m a year, a temptation is to consider the cost to be £120 per unit. This is not reality, however. The reality is that each unit is still using resources with a value of £100 but there are unused resources with a cost of £0.8m. Spreading the cost of unused resource on remaining throughput does not solve the problem, it only hides it, and may send the wrong signal to managers about cost recovery. Highlighting the cost of unused capacity as a separate item of costs sends a clear signal that either more volume has to be found or the cost of the process reduced, if that is possible.

Creating activity costs

There are two main ways of creating activity costs in a business: by starting with general ledger line items or from existing cost centre and department reports. Neither is right or wrong and which to use should depend on the information requirement and the availability of source data. Activity costs from general ledger line items involve the creation of cost pools which bring together all of the relevant costs related to an activity (see Figure 3.8). In this way a suitable means of allocation is devised to share the cost of, say, plant depreciation among all the activities identified in the business as using that resource. As another example, the cost of the payroll department may be allocated based on

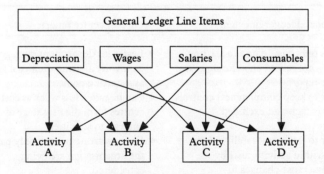

Figure 3.8 Activity costs starting with general ledger line items.

the number of people employed, so each cost pool would pick up a portion of the payroll administration cost based on the number of people allocated to each cost pool.

The second method, using cost centre or department reports, simply takes advantage of the existing analysis of costs before creating activity cost pools, usually in the form of a simple matrix as given in Figure 3.9.

The relative merits of these two approaches are compared in Table 3.1. With either method it is important to be able to retain the integrity of the cost build-up within the activity costs. This is because, for activity costs to be useful, it is necessary to be able to differentiate between the elements of cost within the activity cost; some of these will vary in the short term with changes to the level of activity and some will not. In

Department Cost Report				
	Activity 1	Activity 2	Activity 3	Activity, etc. 4
Salaries	✘	✘		✘
Wages		✘	✘	✘
Depreciation	✘	✘	✘	✘
Consumables	✘		✘	
etc.	✘	✘	✘	✘
TOTAL	✘	✘	✘	✘

Figure 3.9 Activity costs based on existing cost centre or department reports.

Table 3.1 A comparison of activity costing based on general ledger line items and on cost centre reports.

From general ledger line item	From cost centre reports
• Needs only basic data as a starting point – not reliant on accurate cost centre reports.	• Easier for department managers to be involved, using their cost reports as a starting point.
• Easier to keep completeness controls on costs included/excluded.	• Can be much less work as cost centres form the first stage of analysis to activities.
• Easier to retain traceability of the costs within activity costs by avoiding cross-changes to departments *then* to activities.	• Easier starting point if only parts of the organisation are being considered.

Figure 3.10 the cost of computer usage is an allocation from the computer department and will in itself be made up of a number of different types of cost. Software packages are now available and systems are being built which enable a **full** explosion of activity costs to be made, so that an activity cost can be broken down into the different elements of cost within it, irrespective of which department the cost was incurred in. The different types of cost within an activity cost can then be viewed to assess their various patterns of spending behaviour. This means that when, for example, a product cost is built up with many activities, the activity costs can be sorted into the different cost types, to facilitate a better understanding of the impact of changes to product volume on cost behaviour.

Cost drivers

The term **cost driver** has been in use for a long time and has been strongly associated with the recent interest in activity-based approaches. There has, however, been little consistency over what is meant by the term. One of the earlier uses was by Robin Cooper when using activity costs for product costing. He coined the term **first stage cost driver** as a way of getting costs from a general ledger line item to an activity cost pool and **second stage cost driver** to get the activity cost onto the product. This is illustrated in Figure 3.11. Thus first stage cost drivers in

| Computer Usage |
| Supervision |
| Telephone |
| Wages |
| Office Space |
| Consumables |

Figure 3.10 Activity cost: processing of domestic sales order.

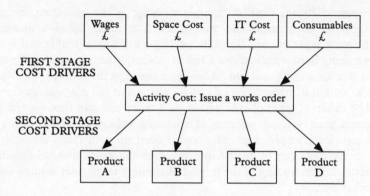

Figure 3.11 The cost of issuing a works order.

this use of the term comprise factors such as time spent, floor area, etc. (in a similar way that costs are often spread to department cost centres for budgetary control), and the second stage cost driver links the activity cost to the product; in Figure 3.11, the number of works orders needed for each product.

While the use of first and second stage cost drivers is useful in the context given, there is another dimension to the use of the term cost driver; these being the factors which cause so **much** cost to occur when an activity takes place, rather than the factor which causes the activity to occur so often. The 'Y' diagram of Figure 3.12 acknowledges there will be factors that determine how often the activity takes place, which are the activity level drivers. Thus a large product range made up of many

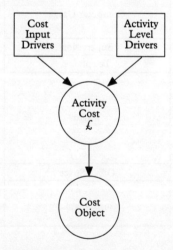

Figure 3.12 The factors that cause cost to occur.

subassemblies will drive a high level of the activity 'issue works order', and if product costing is the objective of the exercise, this cost needs to be linked to products in accordance with the number of works orders they require. The cost input drivers, however, are the factors which cause the activity of 'issue works order' to cost as much as it does when it takes place. Such factors might include the forms and procedures being used, the motivation, skill and ability of the staff involved and the accuracy of the records and data they receive from other departments. It may be that the organisation wishes to **increase** the number of works orders, so that batch sizes can be reduced in an effort to reduce lead-times and increase flexibility, and this emphasises the need, then, to understand the cost input drivers so that the activities can be carried out more effectively, or more often, for the same or less cost. This subject is returned to in Chapter 9 'Process improvement'.

Cost layers

Costing systems have a variety of uses such as decision support, control and planning. The essential point for all these uses is that a costing system attempts to model how costs behave. Variables are fed into the system, and the models predict how costs will behave or should have behaved. The closer the costing model is to the reality of the business, the more useful it will be. It is for this reason that activity-based approaches have been so well received. A walk around an office or factory will reveal people carrying out activities and this is how the resources within the business are being used. Activity-based approaches to cost management can be used to build cost models which reflect the significant activities in the business so that when the variable factors in the model are changed the outcome is more meaningful.

The use of activity costs will not, however, give the costing system a structure and it is here that the use of **cost layers** is important. Cost layers are closely linked to the earlier discussion of cost drivers. If the structure of the costing system is to reflect reality, then it must acknowledge the major cost drivers in the business.

This layered approach to creating a costing model contrasts with a **fully absorbed** product costing system, where the implicit assumption is that if product volumes change, then costs will change accordingly. This is clearly not the case. What then does drive cost? An analysis of the cost within a pharmaceutical manufacturing plant revealed the features shown in Table 3.2. Thus only 10% of the costs were driven in accordance with

Table 3.2 An analysis of cost
within a pharmaceutical
manufacturing plant.

	% cost total site
Site-sustaining	12
Process-sustaining	41
Product-sustaining	19
Batch volume	18
Product volume	10
(excluded direct materials)	100

the **volume** of product. A further 18% of cost was driven by the number of **batches** (the industry requires long clean-downs and set-ups). The cost of **sustaining** the product range in the business (product specifications, test procedures, product records, etc.) accounted for 19% of the cost. Thus, whatever happened to product volume and the number of batches made, this cost would only change with the number of products in the product range. The largest single element of cost was to sustain the **processes** in the business. This was the cost of the plant and infrastructure for the manufacturing process. These costs only go away if the process is no longer carried out. Finally, there are site-sustaining costs, which only go away if the site is closed down (site security, buildings, rates, etc.).

Having built up costs in such layers it is of course possible to collapse them down to the product level but the resulting product costs are only valid if all the relationships between layers remain constant in the cost model.

So far only product-related costs have been considered. The second main cost structure within a business usually concerns customer-driven costs. Here the cost layers may follow a pattern such as the one in Figure 3.13. There will be costs driven by the volume of sales orders (which are irrespective of the value of the order) and costs driven by the delivery volume. These costs will be specific to customers and there will be costs specific to sustaining the customer as a customer (sales visits, customer records, credit control). There will also be the costs of being in a market segment, which are irrespective of the activities of the customers in that segment (preparing a price list, advertising, trade fairs). Again, when these costs are built up in layers, they reflect the reality of how costs behave.

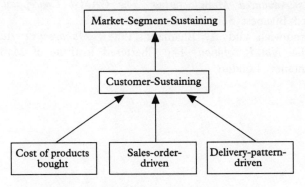

Figure 3.13 Cost layers for customer-driven costs.

As well as constructing cost layers for product-driven activities and customer-driven activities, there will also be costs to sustain the business. Thus the cost of the managing director, of preparing monthly accounts and the audit will only go away if the business no longer exists.

Creating the appropriate cost layers is the key to any costing system if it is to reflect reality and provide useful information. Their use is further explored in Chapters 4 and 5.

Future uses of activity-based approaches

This chapter gives just an overview of the principles of activity-based approaches. Already, in a short time, they have become widely used, and experience has rapidly advanced knowledge of how and when they are effective. As for the future, it is likely that ABC will become less of an issue and will not be seen as an objective in its own right. Instead, activity-based approaches will become an accepted technique to help achieve better and more meaningful information in a number of applications, whether product costing, budgeting or process improvement. It is on this basis that activity-based techniques are described in the following chapters of this book.

References

1 Robin Cooper and Robert Kaplan (1991), *The Design of Cost Management Systems: Text, Cases and Readings*, Prentice Hall: Englewood Cliffs, NJ
2 Callie Berliner and James A. Brimson (eds), *Cost Management for*

Today's Advanced Manufacturing: The CAM-I Conceptual Design, Harvard Business School Press: Boston, MA

3 M. Bromwich and A. Bhamani (1988), *Management Accounting: Evolution Not Revolution*, The Chartered Institute of Management Accountants: London

CHAPTER 4

Product costing

There is a strong argument that manufacturing companies have suffered in the past by allowing their cost reporting systems to be concentrated unduly on product cost information. Many of the most important and exciting developments in performance measurement and cost management in recent years have taken the focus elsewhere, principally onto some of the other subjects covered in this book, including profitability analysis, operational control, process improvement, budgeting and cost reporting. These developments have served not to discredit product costing as a management tool but to place it in its proper context. In identifying where product costing is not appropriate, it is also easier to see where it is.

This chapter deals with the changing uses of product costing, how these have evolved, and the influences on this change, notably activity-based approaches, layered cost reporting and target costing.

Changing uses of product cost information

Traditionally, there have been three particularly widespread uses of product cost information. The usefulness of each of these has to be seriously considered in a modern business environment. They are as follows:

• **Inventory valuation for financial accounts**: It has already been argued in Chapter 2 that in many manufacturing companies the management accounting system has been made subservient to financial accounting requirements. This has been widely attributed to the importance placed on external financial reporting in Western economies. Accounting standards require inventory to be valued in total, but do not lay down any requirements for meaningful valuation by individual product or product group. Consequently, little importance has been placed on a realistic allocation of costs between individual products, and many costing systems are poorly equipped to achieve this.

- **Basis for standard costing variance reporting**: Product costs often form the basis of four very widely used measures, material usage variance, machine utilisation, direct labour usage and overhead recovery. The first three of these have a limited value in giving some sort of overall financial operational control although, as Chapters 7 and 8 demonstrate, they do not present the whole story; the fourth measure, overhead recovery, can give a dangerously misleading message.

- **Support for pricing decisions**: Businesses have sought to achieve an acceptable level of return by reference to the product cost plus a profit margin, either to set a price or to decide if the product is worth making in view of the price set by market conditions. Yet the notion that indirect costs vary largely with product volume is often unfounded.

When considering these uses, it is important to consider the make-up of product costs. The higher the element of direct costs, the more relevant is their use for variance analysis **for the direct element of cost** and also for pricing decision support. Thus, businesses which have products with a large cost represented by raw materials, components, direct labour, consumables, energy and packaging will need to focus on accounting for such costs and measuring their use. There are many such businesses.

The treatment of direct costs brings its own issues, mainly surrounding rising and falling price levels and the resulting need for last-in-first-out (LIFO), first-in-first-out (FIFO), average costing (AVCO) and next-in-first-out (NIFO) techniques. These issues are not new, however, and do not warrant further discussion here.

Production labour often forms a grey area between direct and indirect cost categories. The introduction of automation and cell manufacturing has added to this confusion. It is rare for the **spending** pattern of labour costs to vary exactly with unit volume unless piece payments form the largest element of pay. There are, however, still many businesses where the requirement for operatives is driven principally by unit volume, and this cost forms a large part of total cost. In these cases it is appropriate to treat the cost as a direct cost, if such treatment is accompanied by an understanding that the spending will not change with short term unit volume changes. In such businesses the distinction still has to be drawn between direct operators and supervisors, setters, foremen, etc., whose activities will not be driven by unit volume. The division of labour between direct and indirect is one which therefore has to be drawn carefully to reflect the circumstances of the business.

Of greater interest is the treatment of indirect costs, that is, those costs where the resource consumption and resulting spending do not vary directly with product volume. As described in Chapter 2, in many manufacturing businesses it is this element of cost which has grown considerably in recent years and where traditional approaches to variance analysis and pricing decision support do not reflect reality.

The way in which product cost information (where indirect costs are included) is traditionally reported gives a message, both to management and to other staff, that costs can be controlled as a direct result of managing product volumes and mix. There are countless cases where the expected cost savings resulting from a plan of action have not been achieved because the plan was based upon false assumptions about the way in which costs actually behave – either because it was assumed that more costs would go away with a reduction in volume than in fact turned out to be the case, or because costs increased even faster than anticipated when volumes rose.

Furthermore, there has long been a tendency to confuse costing and pricing. This is exacerbated by the financial-accounting-inspired use of fully absorbed (or near fully absorbed) product costs. The reality is that costs are driven by many different factors within a business and as a result of different influences. Recognition of this leads to a realisation that the question: 'How much does it cost us to make product X?' is, for most businesses, unanswerable – or, at best, the answer would have to be heavily qualified. Even if the question is turned to: 'What costs would we save if we stopped making product X?', the answer would probably be: 'It depends over what time period you are looking.' Table 4.1 illustrates this point. This table shows the link between resource consumption and spending for the resources concerned.[1] In the very short term the only saving from lower product volumes in addition to raw materials and machine power may be overtime and piece payments. If volumes were to fall low enough, it may be possible to take out direct and indirect labour and, ultimately, to close a facility. However, just because all spending does not change directly with resource consumption, this does not invalidate the need to understand these costs. The cost of using the resource of machine-time (even though the spending has already taken place) is the opportunity that is lost for another product to use it. Management should be concerned with maximising the return from all the resources at its disposal.

However, for the person asking the question: 'How much does it cost us to make product X?', a more answerable question might be: 'What is the minimum we must recover when selling product X in order to make an acceptable return for the company?' Part of the problem in the

Table 4.1 The link between resource consumption and spending on those resources.

Type of resource	Spending trigger	Time lag
Piece-rate payments	Activity level	Immediate
Machine power	↓	↓
Overtime	↓	1 week
Direct labour	Discretionary	1–3 months
Indirect labour	↓	3–6 months
Rent	↓	6–12 months
Plant	Historic	—

confusion between costing and pricing is that traditional product costs give misleading implications about how costs behave. They do not separate those costs that vary with volume of product from those which are dependent on the number of batches run, the number of product lines being made, or the number of sites operated and other cost layers. This approach leads into thinking about how costs behave and into the use of cost layers.[2] Considering a **layered cost recovery model** moves away from a cost-plus mind-set and, even more importantly, acknowledges that many of the costs incurred in the business are not directly attributable to the products themselves.

A simple example can be used to demonstrate the above point. Consider a business that manufactures four products. The total cost base is £5m and the costs in this case can be broken down into five layers such as those in Table 4.2. The first three layers, totalling £3m can all be driven directly to one of the four products. The volumes and activity-based costs of each product are shown in Table 4.3. This still leaves £2m unaccounted for. (This £2m will itself comprise several cost layers, but

Table 4.2 An example of cost layers for a manufacturing business.

	£m
Business-sustaining	1.5
Site-sustaining	0.5
Product-volume-related	1.5
Batch-volume-related	0.5
Product-sustaining	1.0
Total	5.0

Table 4.3 Volumes and activity-based costs by product.

Product	A	B	C	D	Total
Product cost (£)	100	150	200	50	
Volume manufactured	8,000	6,000	2,500	16,000	32,000
Total product cost (£)	800,000	900,000	500,000	800,000	3,000,000

these have been ignored for the purposes of this illustration.) Since this £2m represents costs such as administration, general management, systems, site security, personnel and many others, any attempt to relate these to individual products has to be arbitrary. The issue for management is to achieve a return for the company that is satisfactory – and to ensure that each of the four products is pulling its weight in achieving that return.

Let us now assume that management has little influence over the price it can charge, all four products being in a market-driven pricing environment. The market price for each product is given in Table 4.4. Assuming that all units manufactured could be sold at these prices, the contribution for each product would be assessed as in Table 4.5. The total contribution is £2.6m which, after other costs of £2m, leaves a company profit of £0.6m.

Products A, B and D are all contributing to profit. Product C may still be establishing itself in the market, or it may be a loss leader, or it may

Table 4.4 Price set for each product
in a market-driven environment.

Product	A	B	C	D
Price (£)	150	200	175	175

Table 4.5 The contribution from each product towards the company.

Product	A	B	C	D	Total
Revenue (£000)	1,200	1,200	437.5	2,800	5,637
Product cost (£000)	800	900	500	800	3,000
Contribution (£000)	400	300	(62.5)	2,000	2,637.5

be genuinely unprofitable and management may wish to consider various courses of action to correct this situation. In any event management will be able to look at the activities needed within each layer of cost to see if the process can be improved to reduce the manufacturing cost.

Now, consider what might happen if, instead of looking at contribution, management took decisions on the basis of a fully absorbed product cost (see Table 4.6). While the total profit figure obviously does not change, Products A and B now appear unprofitable. It is unlikely that any management in such a simple situation would be naive enough to fall into a 'vicious spiral' by concluding that Product D is its only profitable product, pulling out of everything else but then finding that costs do not go with the products. However, in an environment where the product range numbers hundreds or thousands, less clear-cut decisions can easily be taken on such a basis. In this example, even if all the direct labour and materials costs attributable to Products A, B and C could be saved – which is by no means necessarily the case – Product D would still have to recover £2m of site and business-sustaining cost.

In the first case, however, there is **visibility** as to what the structure of their business is, the factors driving costs and the resulting cost layers. This will enable management to question cost levels and ask what needs to be done to get costs down. In the second case, management are no wiser about the cost structure of their business, other than understanding direct costs and global allocations based on machine-time.

So far, the use of product costs has been considered in the context of:

● understanding the link between resource consumption and changes in spending; and
● building up costs in layers so that only product-related costs are included, and important cost drivers other than product volumes are recognised.

Table 4.6 Assessing the viability of products on the basis of fully absorbed product cost.

Product (£000)	A	B	C	D	Total
Raw materials	300	200	100	200	800
Direct labour	200	200	100	200	700
Machine-hour Overhead burden	900	1,100	700	800	3,500
Total cost	1,400	1,500	900	1,200	5,000
Revenue	1,200	1,200	438	2,800	5,638
Profit/loss	(200)	(300)	(462)	1,600	638

Now, the link between products and the resources they consume will be explored through the use of activity-based approaches.

Activity-based product costing

Briefly, the difference between the traditional approach to product costing and an activity-based approach is illustrated in Figures 4.1 and 4.2. Figure 4.1 shows a simple and typical allocation basis for taking overheads to products, related to the number of direct labour or machine-hours spent making the product. Figure 4.2 demonstrates an approach that takes account of the different activities needed to make the product and which drives cost to product on the basis of how much of each resource is consumed by the activities performed in making each product. This figure effectively demonstrates what activity-based product costing is. It is no more and no less than a more meaningful way of understanding the way in which resources are consumed in manufacturing a product. If resources are not devoted specifically to manufacturing a product, they are not taken into account at the product level. An activity-based product costing model will not automatically tell management how to cut costs, nor will it necessarily show which product to cut, which to keep, which to expand and how much to sell it for. Like any management tool, it is likely to provoke as many questions as it answers.

Figures 4.3 and 4.4 give an example of a typical activity-based product cost with, alongside it, the traditionally-reported cost for the same product. The difference in total cost can be explained, broadly, by one or both of the following reasons.

Firstly, the costs that have been treated as falling within the product cost boundary could have changed. It is common practice in many manufacturing companies for the factory floor to be treated as the product cost boundary: all costs incurred within that boundary are included, all those outside are excluded. Yet some activities performed outside that boundary are directly related to product; examples may include production planning and scheduling and certain materials handling functions. Equally, the factory floor boundary may well include activities which are not product-related at all. As part of the layered approach to costing, activities are reported according to the level of the business that they help to **sustain**, rather than on the basis of where they happen to be **incurred**.

The second reason for a change in the product cost is, simply, that the more meaningful cost model provided by an activity-based approach reflects the fact that, as the examples used earlier in this chapter showed,

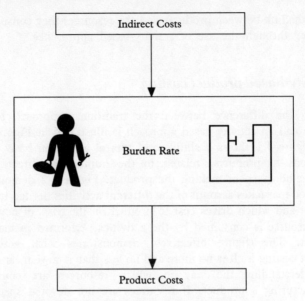

Figure 4.1 Volume-based cost drivers fail to reflect diversity of resource consumption.

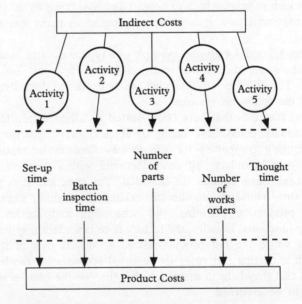

Figure 4.2 Understanding activities and cost drivers creates a meaningful link between products and the resources they consume.

Activity-Based Product Cost							
Set-up	Inspection	Expediting	Scheduling	Picking	Direct Labour	Direct Materials	Activity
Number of Batches	Number of Inspections	Cell Throughput Time	Number of Works Orders	Number of Parts	—	—	Cost Driver
10.00	12.50	16.25	10.00	5.75	10.50	12.00	£

Total cost: £77.00

Figure 4.3 A typical activity-based product cost.

Traditional Product Cost			
Overhead	Direct Labour	Direct Materials	Cost Category
35.50	10.50	12.00	£

Total cost: £58.00

Figure 4.4 The traditional product cost for the same example as Figure 4.3.

some products are responsible for the consumption of more resource than others.

Thus, an activity-based approach recognises **diversity** of resource consumption. A machine-hour overhead burden rate only recognises (and amplifies the effect of) the diversity of machine-hour use. An activity-based approach recognises diversity for however many cost drivers are recognised in the costing system. So the products that cause more work orders, inspection, parts handling, etc., are costed accordingly. In particular activity-based product costs recognise the cost of complexity. Complexity may be caused by the number of products in the product range, by the number of components, the nature of the production processes or any other causes. Activity-based product costing therefore typically takes cost away from high volume easy-to-make products and puts it onto complex, difficult-to-make products.

There are two obvious issues of concern to companies who recognise their own situation in the analysis above. Firstly, what are the practicalities of generating activity-based information? And, secondly and most critically, what impact – if any – will the generation of such information have on the way in which the business is run? Any proposed change to the way in which information is reported must be seen to be capable of passing the 'so what?' test before it is implemented. The remainder of this section deals with the question of practicality. The next section, 'Future uses of product costing', addresses the issue of usefulness.

Taking the question of practicality, it is obviously true that the greater and more wide-ranging the data requirement, the more the effort that will be needed to be invested in collecting and manipulating it. However, the decision facing management is not as simple as finding an appropriate point on the spectrum in terms of the compromise between accuracy of information generated and the investment of time, resource and money required to generate that information. Management must establish what type of information it needs, to what degree of accuracy that information should go, how frequently that information should be produced and what management will do with it when it receives it. Beyond a certain degree of accuracy, nothing further can be added to the value of the information produced. The relevant degree of accuracy depends on the nature of the decision that the information is helping a manager to take, and to an extent on the individual style of the manager or managers.

In common with any information review, therefore, the starting point must be to ask: 'Why are we collecting this data and reporting this information?' For the purposes of product costing, the balance of resource required versus accuracy can sometimes be established by piloting a small area of the business and performing a sensitivity analysis at the margin for the effect on reported product costs on the introduction or removal of one activity or cost driver. If the introduction of one additional activity (which otherwise would have been treated as a subsidiary part of a more widely defined activity) makes little or no difference to reported product cost, there is no point in reporting it separately. The example below illustrates this.

The information in Table 4.7 is obtained concerning an activity in a manufacturing cell. Upon further enquiry, the inspection activity is found to comprise two discrete stages: general quality assurance and

Table 4.7 Details of an activity in a manufacturing cell.

Activity	Inspection
Driver:	No. of items made
Activity cost:	£25,000.00
Driver volume:	5,000
Cost per item:	£5.00

first-piece inspection. The time spent on first-piece inspection is approximately 40% of the total and the first-piece inspection activity is found to cost £10,000, whilst general quality assurance costs £15,000.

There are now two activities, each with its own driver, with the features shown in Table 4.8. Cost per item depends on the batch size. At this point, the example can be split into two scenarios.

In Scenario 1, the average batch size is found to vary considerably. The average batch size is one hundred but this may vary between one and a thousand. For product-costing purposes, an item in a batch of 1 should be loaded with more cost than one in a batch of a thousand because the decision to make that product, and to do so in so small a batch size, was responsible for a whole inspection being performed. Therefore in this example, the first-piece inspection unit cost of an item in a batch of one, a hundred and a thousand respectively would be as given in Table 4.9.

In Scenario 2, the average batch size is very consistent. The average is again a hundred but the actual never varies outside the range 95 to 105. Calculated in the same way, the first-piece inspection unit cost of an item in a small, average and large batch respectively would follow Table 4.10.

In both scenarios, a comparison must be drawn with the unit inspection cost of £5.00 that would have been achieved if only one

Table 4.8 Considering the activity of Table 4.7 as two activities.

Activity 1	General QA	Activity 2	First-piece inspection
Driver:	No. of items made	Driver:	No. of batches
Activity cost:	£15,000.00	Activity cost:	£10,000.00
Driver volume:	5,000	Driver volume:	50
Cost per item:	£3.00	Cost per batch:	£200.00
		Cost per item:	See below

Table 4.9 The cost of first-piece inspection for varying batch sizes.

Product	A	B	C
Cost per batch	£200	£200	£200
No. of items in batch	1	100	1,000
First-piece inspection cost per item	£200.00	£2.00	£0.20
General QA cost per item	£3.00	£3.00	£3.00
Total unit inspection costs	£203.00	£5.00	£3.20

Table 4.10   The cost of inspection for batch sizes of smaller variation.

Product	A	B	C
Cost per batch	£200	£200	£200
No. of items in batch	95	100	105
First-piece inspection cost per item	£2.10	£2.00	£1.90
General QA cost per item	£3.00	£3.00	£3.00
Total unit inspection costs	£5.10	£5.00	£4.90

inspection activity had been used. In Scenario 2, it would probably not be worth identifying and processing another activity because the impact on unit product cost is so small. In Scenario 1 this is not the case. The costs of the two activities behave in significantly different ways because of the diversity in driver volumes, and it would therefore be appropriate to split the inspection activity into two.

Typically, the first stage in an activity-based product costing exercise is to undertake an analysis to establish for the area in question (which could be a whole factory or a pilot area) setting out:

● The levels of costs that will be recognised
● Main activities
● Related cost drivers
● First-cut activity cost
● Cost driver volumes (if available)
● Cost per unit of driver

Although such an analysis will contain some approximations and unsubstantiated assumptions at this stage, it is a very helpful first pass at identifying the major activities in the factory, and for focusing attention on two points in particular: low cost activities that may be capable of being merged with others, and driver volume data that might be difficult to obtain. In the latter case it is necessary either to find another driver, if one can be identified, or to establish some means of approximating the driver volumes that cannot be precisely captured (a surrogate driver).

To illustrate how to deal with a driver that cannot be directly measured, an example can be taken from a food processing company which found that a significant activity in preparing for a processing run was moving bags of ingredients from one part of the factory to another, for example, from one hopper to another or from the raw materials store to the factory floor. There was, however, no practical means of measuring the **number of times** a bag was moved, so after some discussion it was agreed that, since each bag carried a different ingredient, and there was no apparent characteristic that meant that bags containing some ingredients needed to be moved any more frequently than others, it would be a reasonable approximation to drive the cost of the bag-moving activity to products on the basis of the number of raw material ingredients in the product. This had the double advantage of using, as driver volume data, information that was both readily available and was already being used as a driver for other activities.

A second example relates to a situation where the cost driver was reasonably clearly understood but it could not be directly quantified. This problem arose in the materials handling process of an engineering company. Discussion with staff and managers who were either involved in or benefited from the purchasing, goods inwards and stores activities threw out the following information:

- The company's materials purchases broadly fell into three categories: steel, subassemblies and consumables.
- Steel accounted for about 70% in value terms of the materials purchased.
- The most time-consuming purchase orders to handle were the one-off steel orders, which were generally for low value and low volume items.
- The easiest orders to deal with, especially in the purchasing activity, were the higher volume steel items, for which a call-off contract had been established with suppliers. Since most of the paperwork and contractual arrangements had been handled in advance, organising a delivery was straightforward. Although a lot of this product was bought, ordering it consisted of little more than picking up the telephone and having a brief conversation with the supplier's sales order processing department.

It would have been misleading to have used a driver for this activity such as weight or value of materials, as this would have given completely the wrong message about what was causing cost and complexity within the business. The solution that was finally agreed is set out in Table 4.11.

Staff engaged in each of the purchasing, goods inwards and stores activities were asked to analyse how much time they spent dealing with each type of material. The cost of each activity was then split between material types according to the percentages obtained. So, for example, only 5% of purchasing time was spent ordering high volume steel, and the cost of this activity was therefore 5% of the total purchasing cost of £160,000 = £8,000. Purchasing consumables, on the other hand, took up 30% of the staff's time and the cost was therefore £48,000.

Table 4.11   Assessing the cost of materials handling.

	Purchasing (% time spent)	Goods inwards Stores (% time spent)	Stores (% time spent)	Purchasing (£000)	Goods inwards (£000)	Stores (£000)	Total cost (£000)	Material value (£000)	Activity (% cost per £ value)
Steel:									
● high volume	5	10	15	8	20	36	64	4,000	1.6%
● medium volume	20	15	20	32	30	48	110	1,500	7.3%
● low volume	20	15	25	32	30	60	122	1,500	8.1%
Subassemblies	25	30	20	40	60	48	148	2,000	7.4%
Consumables	30	30	20	48	60	48	156	1,000	15.6%
	100	100	100	160	200	240	600	10,000	

The next stage was to add up the total cost of all materials handling activities relating to each type of material. This is shown in the total cost column. This is then related to the total value of the material purchased to get to an activity cost per £ value of material purchased. It is this figure which is used to drive materials handling cost down to product; in the case of low volume steel, for example, for every £1 of material consumed by a particular product an additional 8.1 pence will be added to the product cost to reflect the amount of overhead consumed in handling the material compared to 1.6% for high volume. Thus, the products using the extra resource used to purchase low volume steel are costed accordingly. The approach captured the essential diversity of resource consumption between products.

An engineering components manufacturer, which adopted activity-based product costing, illustrates some interesting points referred to so far. The company sells into three market sectors, one of which, the automotive sector, is considerably larger in sales than either of the other two. The sales manager responsible for automotive customers was a particularly keen supporter of an activity-based costing exercise because he was convinced that his market was more profitable than the existing costing system suggested. Indeed, so bleak was the reported position that the board was seriously considering withdrawing from automotive business altogether.

One reason that the automotive business appeared relatively unprofit-able was that it tended to be run in high volume batches which were unfairly burdened with the costs incurred in running the many small batches for other products. Batch-related costs (such as set-up, first-off inspection, some production planning and works order costs) were very significant at this company, accounting for some 20% of indirect product costs. Under the traditional costing system, these costs, like all other manufacturing overheads, were driven down to products on the basis of machine-hours. Therefore an automotive component that formed part of a batch of 1,000 and required one hour of machine-time would absorb as much overhead as another product that also took one hour to machine but which was made in a batch size of ten.

The activity-based product costing system provided a new perspective. If all costs driven by the number of batches were £100 per batch, the cost per unit in a batch of 1,000 would be £0.10. On the other hand, the cost per unit in a batch of 10 was £10. This effect was one of the main reasons why the automotive sector appeared far more profitable than it had previously and, far from withdrawing, management made a renewed commitment to it. Since, under the old system, much of the cost associated with non-automotive products had been transferred to automotive products, withdrawal would simply have meant that proportionately more overhead had to be absorbed by a much smaller volume of product, so that products which had previously appeared to be profitable would now have been loss-makers; and so the vicious spiral could have continued.

The analysis also helped management to better understand the costs driven by the number of batches which had been a long-standing management concern. It had been difficult in the past to support this concern with numbers because there was no way of extracting the relevant information from the costing system. Batch-related activities were performed by a whole range of people, including staff from both the direct and indirect categories. The issue was a particularly important one because of management's commitment to reducing batch sizes (thus increasing the number of batches) to enhance flexibility on the factory floor.

When first-pass activity costs were produced, management fears were confirmed. Almost 12% of total factory overhead was being driven by the number of batches. A review of cost input drivers (see Chapter 3) was put into place immediately with a view to reducing the number of aborted set-ups, maximising partial changeovers and ensuring that set-ups were performed by appropriately trained staff. Among the other main causes of the high batch-related cost was the large number of interruptions to the schedule, and the failure to have materials in the right place at the right time. These were addressed through improving the associated processes. Thus the activity-based approach did not provide answers to problems but gave **visibility** to the issues and quantified costs in such a way that management were triggered into taking action. Experience shows, time and time again, that activity-based approaches are very effective in quantifying and highlighting issues in a way that encourages management to take action.

Future uses of product costing

Arguably, the future role of product costing is concerned with looking forwards, not just backwards, and for process improvement. Traditional approaches to product costing cannot often achieve these objectives; the change in the way product costs should be used has to be preceded by a change in the way indirect costs are captured, analysed and reported. The impact of activity-based approaches to product costing has in this respect been very significant.

The role of product costing in the future is likely to be in the following areas:

● Continuing to provide support for tactical pricing decisions
● Identifying causes of resource consumption and ways of saving resource, particularly at the product and process design stage
● Longer term strategic product investment and resource deployment decisions, and understanding market profitability

Product costs will continue to play an important part of tactical pricing support. To the extent that product costs comprise direct costs, this is essential. It has to be remembered, also, that not many businesses can set prices purely by reference to competitors and the market. In these cases a reference to the usage of indirect costs at the product level is an important element to support the pricing decision (but not to determine them). The problem with using product costs with a high degree of indirect cost arises in this context when, as has been explained, there is an expectation that they represent a **short term** model of cost behaviour, which is rarely the case.

Moving on to the second point listed above, it was suggested in Chapter 1 that most manufacturing costs (a figure of 85% was given) are determined at the product design stage, including the influence that product design has on process-driven costs. It is here that the greatest savings in manufacturing cost can be achieved. It is increasingly the trend in forward-thinking and high-performing companies from America for finance staff to become involved in product and process design, working alongside design staff to model the financial implications of design decisions and to ensure, together, that the final outcome is both functionally and financially acceptable. It is this use of looking forwards, not backwards, where product costing has greatest potential. Further-more, an activity basis of building up product costs lends itself ideally to this use, as the cost of indirect resources used is identified and visible.

Using product costing techniques at the design stage links straight to target costing. This technique, developed and widely used in Japan, involves starting with a predicted selling price in the market for a product with a defined functionality. The required profit margin is then deducted to arrive at a target cost. The designer then has to attempt to design the product so it can be made for that cost. Furthermore it is possible to optimise profitability by balancing the features of the product (expressed as value to the customer in terms of how much he will pay for them) against the cost of those features.

The use of product costing at the design stage can also have a direct behaviourial effect. In a well-known case study of Tektronix Portable Instrument Division,[3] the designers of oscilloscopes kept adding to the range of components used in the business as each new machine they designed contained many new components to suit the designers' technical requirements. Activity analysis revealed that about half of all indirect cost was concerned with the components; this included buying, storing and handling them. The size of the component range was the major contributor to this cost. Tektronix decided to introduce an overhead 'head tax' to each component. In this way each **type** of component number had to bear an overhead charge for the year, which represented the overhead cost of sustaining that component in the business. This overhead charge was then divided by the usage of the component.

Thus high volume components had a low unit overhead, whereas low volume components had a high unit charge. When designers designed new machines they had to meet a target cost which included a component overhead on the basis described. Naturally, they tended to use the high volume components if that was practical. Over time, this had the effect of solving the component range proliferation problem through natural selection by the design engineers.

The third use of product costs listed above, for strategic investment and resource development, is one where activity-based techniques have particularly added a great deal of benefit through creating a better understanding of the drivers of indirect cost. The essence of this use is to be able to match what the business is good at doing to where the greatest value is created for the product in the marketplace.

Thus product costs reflect the use of resource by the business and market prices reflect the value customers put on those products. In this way product costs can be used to assess profitability by product group, customer type or whatever is appropriate. Having understood this the business can be focused on areas of greatest return. (This view is often further enhanced by also considering customer-driven costs, as described in the next chapter.) Alternatively, the build-up of product costs can show how the business needs to change if it is to be competitive in the markets it is aiming for. This could concern, for example, understanding how far cost levels have to fall when benchmarked against the lowest cost producer in the sector. Alternatively the option being considered may comprise subcontracting an element of manufacture previously made in-house, or greatly rationalising the product range, to gain the advantages of being a focused factory, and badge engineering from other suppliers to complete the product range.

In all these uses product costs are performing a strategic level model of the business and decision-making from such a view will need to reflect appropriate timescales.

In conclusion, therefore, despite rumours to the contrary, product costing is still very much alive. Its future worth, however, depends primarily on companies' ability to define its predominantly strategic place in the overall business management framework. This in turn will clarify the relationship of product costing to the other, more focused cost management tools described elsewhere in this book.

References

1 R. Cooper and R. Kaplan (1991), Profit priorities from activity based costing, *Harvard Business Review*, vol. 69, no. 3, pp. 130–5
2 R. Cooper (1990), Cost classification in unit based and activity based manufacturing cost systems, *Journal of Cost Management*, vol. 4, no. 3, pp. 4–14
3 R. Cooper and P. Turney (1988), *Tektronix: Portable Instruments Division*, Harvard Business School reference 9–188–143, 144 and 145

CHAPTER 5

Profitability analysis

In the last chapter the development of product costing was explored and it was concluded that its role today is significantly different from that which it has played historically. Its contribution is primarily at the strategic level, and it is often inappropriate to use product cost information, generated to support strategic decisions, as a sole basis for trying to manage profitability. As the role of product costing changes so does its content; in order for it to become more relevant it has been necessary for product cost information to reflect more meaningfully the various resources consumed in making that product. This value is lost, however, if an attempt is made to drive down to products the costs of those activities which are unrelated to the amount of product being made. But these costs remain very relevant to cost recovery and pricing decisions.

This chapter therefore addresses the question: If product costs are to fulfil the role identified for them in the previous chapter, what happens to the other costs of the business?

Hierarchical cost reporting

The concept that activities – and therefore costs – are incurred at different layers has been introduced in the previous chapters. Even within product-related costs, the significantly varied behaviour patterns of unit-driven, batch-driven, process-sustaining and product-sustaining costs can be recognised, captured and reported. The same principle applies when looking at the costs of those activities that are not directly related to product.

One of the most common applications of building cost layers beyond product costs is to add revenue values to create profitability analysis. It is important to understand which products are contributing to the long term profitability of the business, but at least as essential is to be able to manage effectively the resources that create customer interest in the product, get the product to the customer, and maintain the relationship with that customer in order to encourage them to come back and buy again. Traditional cost reporting systems have not handled this requirement well, and it is a pertinent point that in many companies the most enthusiastic supporters of new approaches to cost reporting and management are sales and marketing managers, eager to understand more about customer and market segment profitability in particular.

The principle behind reporting such profitability is straightforward, and an example will help to demonstrate how any such hierarchy can be constructed. Figure 5.1 sets out a typical profitability analysis hierarchy, which reports profit at the product, customer order, customer and market segment levels. The profit on each product comprising each sales order is added together. From this profit figure is deducted the activity costs of processing that order. This gives the profitability of the order. Then the profits on all the orders for a particular customer are added up in the same way, and the costs of the activities incurred in supporting that customer are deducted to give customer profitability. The market-segment-specific costs can then be deducted from the combined profitability of all customers in a particular segment. This process is summarised in Figure 5.2. The simple structure shown is not fixed; the layers of costs appropriate to a business, the diversity of cost and the information requirement will all determine an appropriate structure and suitable classification for that business.

An activity basis is an ideal way of understanding the build-up of costs at each of these layers. Thus, **diversity** will be captured. Some customers will place much heavier demands on order processing, picking, packing and delivery resources than others. Other customers may require heavier levels of sales effort and support. Finally, the cost of supporting different

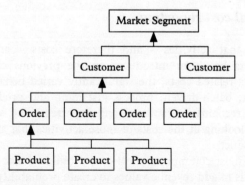

Figure 5.1 Profitability analysis hierarchy.

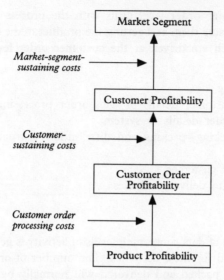

Figure 5.2 Cost levels to support profitability analysis.

market segments will vary. Thus, by using an activity basis, there is a meaningful link between each customer and market segment and the resources they consume. This compares with the arbitrary bases often used in such exercises, where costs are spread on the basis of turnover or volume. Once again, the use of appropriate cost layers and activity costs provides a model of the business which is closer to reflecting the reality of what really happens.

In order to illustrate how this concept is put into practice, the following questions need to be considered:

- What activities are incurred at each level, what analysis is required and how is the relevant cost and non-financial data collected?
- What output is generated?
- How frequently should this output be produced?
- How are profitability reports used?

These questions are addressed below.

Analysis of activities and data capture

In the hierarchy shown in Figures 5.1 and 5.2, three levels of profitability reporting have been identified: order, customer and market segment.

The **customer order** level deals with the process of receiving sales orders, processing them and getting the product to the customer. Typical activities which are driven at the customer order level include:

- Order-taking
- Input of customer details to sales order processing system
- Input of order details to system
- Issue of picking, packing and distribution instructions
- Picking
- Packing for customer
- Loading onto delivery vehicles
- Delivery

The collection of data concerning levels of activity is generally reasonably straightforward for these activities. The number of orders received and items picked, packed and delivered will normally be readily available. Debate is more likely over the possible need to distinguish between the resource required to handle a simple order and a complex one. Some companies have acknowledged that a ten-line order takes longer to enter and process than a one-line order, and have therefore reported a cost per order line as part of order profitability. Others have gone even further, and also incorporated a standing cost per order to take account of the activity that must be performed for every order, regardless of size or complexity: entering of customer name, account number and so on.

Whether these more sophisticated approaches are required to capture order processing costs will depend on such factors as whether:

- A large number of customer orders are received and processed
- The number and complexity of orders received varies widely from one customer to the next (diversity)
- The time and cost involved in entering standing data is significant

Delivery costs present the most difficult data capture and analysis problem at the order profitability level, since it is common for deliveries to involve visits to more than one customer, and the same route may not be followed from one day, or one week, to the next. It is probably true that this issue is less satisfactorily resolved than almost any other, and it is therefore particularly important to remember the trade-off between usefulness and accuracy. The reality of delivery is that it is often not managed on a customer-by-customer basis, but rather as a process, in a way that maximises the value added by the resources involved relative to the cost of those resources.

The options for treatment of delivery costs in a profitability hierarchy include:

- Excluding them altogether
- Including a standard charge per delivery based on distance from point of departure
- Using an algorithm that reflects actual deliveries made and miles travelled

The last option is rarely justifiable, primarily for two reasons: the effort involved is unlikely to be justified for the value of the information and the approach may be inconsistent with the need to manage the delivery process itself. The inclusion of a standard charge is reasonable as an indicator of where resource is being deployed, but it is important to always recognise that the charge made to any particular customer is somewhat artificial. The use of a standard charge per delivery is probably the most common approach, and indeed the most consistent with a cost recovery model. Such a charge is a good example of a cost that would not necessarily go away if that particular delivery were not made.

One business which benefited from order-level profitability analysis was a manufacturing company which distributed products to a large number of customers, both in the United Kingdom and overseas. The key characteristics of the customer base were as follows:

- UK customers ranged from nationwide, multisite retailers through intermediate distributors to small independents; export customers were generally limited to one intermediate distributor in each country.
- Most of the large UK customers ordered centrally but required delivery to each individual site; export orders were normally delivered to the port of departure.
- Most export customers had country-specific product ranges which were much narrower than the general range from which UK customers selected. This had two implications: export orders were generally easier to forecast, and they typically included significantly fewer different products.
- On the other hand, export orders were on average considerably smaller than UK orders, and often involved breaking into batches. This was rarely the case for large UK customers although it did sometimes

apply to the smaller independents. Export orders therefore tended to be smaller and more complex.
● The administration involved in export orders was considerably more complex than for UK orders.

Analysis of the above characteristics identified the key drivers of cost in the order handling process given in Table 5.1. Application of costs to this analysis provided the company's management with support for several key decisions, including:

● The price concessions they could offer to some of the UK chains who were considering switching to central delivery points.
● A basis for negotiation with customers who did not fit the typical profile set out above, for example, distributors who placed several small orders per week.
● Discussion with export customers aimed at achieving a closer fit between projected requirements and the company's manufacturing and stocking levels.

Having considered order level costs, but before going on to customer level costs and market segment costs, it is worth expanding the simple four-level structure shown in Figure 5.2. This is to recognise that some information can be analysed in several different ways (shown here at the market segment level) and also that for some types of analysis (shown here at the product brand level) not all costs may be deducted. In this case it is appropriate to deduct order level costs from product brand groupings, but not to do the same with customer-sustaining costs. Again, the structure which is appropriate will be the one which reflects reality and provides the information needed for decision-making. This ability to be able to slice and analyse the profitability by cost level and by the type of groupings shown in Figure 5.3 can be very powerful indeed and can

Table 5.1 Key drivers of cost in the order handling process.

Driver	Impact			
	UK chains	UK distributors	UK independents	Export
No. of orders	Weekly	Weekly	Monthly	Monthly
No. of products per order	Large	Large	Large	Small
No. of delivery points	Large	Large	Small	Small
Administration	Small	Small	Small	Large
Average order size	Large	Large	Small	Large
Order complexity	Low	Low	Low	High

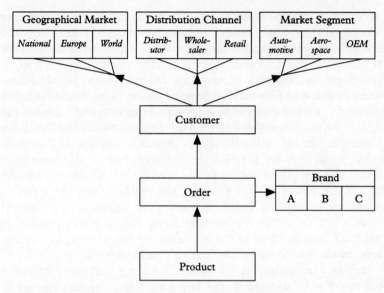

Figure 5.3 Analysing profitability by type of grouping.

give management a new insight into the business. Happily, PC-based software is available which can perform such multidimension analysis with great ease.

Customer level

Although most of the cost driver information required at the order processing level is available either as a matter of course or with little extra effort, this is less likely to be the case at the customer level, where the main relevant activities and costs might be:

- Sales and promotional activities
- Enquiry handling
- Technical support
- Retrospective volume rebates

Although data capture for these costs will be less objective than at the product or order level, the benefits of performing the analysis of causes of resource consumption at customer level are often considerable. Essentially, the requirement is to identify, to the extent that activities are caused by customer demands, the amount of resource that is devoted to each customer. This not only gives an indication of profitability, which helps management to focus attention on whether the resources invested in servicing a customer are generating an acceptable return; it also highlights what type of resource is being consumed in each case and therefore helps management to identify ways in which the same or higher level of service could be delivered more economically or effectively.

To achieve this analysis, salesmen are required to analyse their time between customers. This may be done in greater detail by timesheeting or simply by a sales manager making approximations and a percentage split. If it is possible, depending on what data can be captured, enquiry and complaint handling should also be linked to customers. The main practical issue is likely to relate to the recording of the volume of enquiries and complaints received. The need for this would depend very much on the nature of the business, the product, and the types of enquiries or complaints being received. The approach to technical support is similar to that for the sales force. It is generally possible to obtain from those involved in this area a measure or, at least, an estimate of how much time is spent dealing with each customer.

It may be that analysis is not needed for every customer. Attention would typically be focused on the larger customers, those expected to become large, and any others that appear to be responsible for the consumption of unusually large amounts of resource. Other customers can be consolidated into like groups. An example of a customer profitability reporting format employed by a company in the home decorations market is set out in Figure 5.4.

Figure 5.5 demonstrates the profitability of the same segment analysed by customer type. In this example large customers are reported individually whilst all others in a particular segment – in this case, domestic retailers – are grouped together.

Market segment levels

In the four examples of market segments given in Table 5.1, the cost of typical activities included would relate to:

- Marketing managers
- Price lists
- Advertising and promotion
- Trade shows and exhibitions
- Marketing support and administration

and for the brand level costs:

- Brand managers
- Brand promotional and advertising

	National Accts		Merchants		Key Accts		Other UK		Total UK	
	£K	%	£K	%	£K	%	£K	%	£K	%
Gross sales										
less rebates										
Net sales										
Net margin										
Order level costs										
Salesmen costs										
Pattern book subsidy										
Customer support										
Bad debts										
Samples										
Debt funding										
Specific selling costs										
Contribution										
Market segment level costs										
Net UK contribution										

Figure 5.4 Customer profitability summary report for a home decorations company.

	Total UK £K	%	B&Q £K	%	Texas £K	%	AGS £K	%	Do-It-All £K	%	Homebase £K	%	Other UK Domestic Retailers £K	%
Gross sales														
less rebates														
Net sales														
Net margin														
Order level costs														
Salesmen costs														
Pattern book subsidy														
Customer support														
Bad debts														
Samples														
Debt funding														
Specific selling costs														
Contribution														
Market segment level costs														
Net UK contribution														

Figure 5.5 Customer profitability analysed by customer.

- Technical support costs specific to a brand
- Brand development

These lists obviously cannot be exhaustive. The approach has to be specific to each business.

The product profitability analysis which changed the commitment of an engineering components manufacturer to the automotive sector was described in Chapter 4. This strategic decision was, however, enhanced by the findings of the order, customer and market-segment level analysis within the same company.

Sales and technical support staff were asked to identify how much time they spent supporting each customer or customer group. They were also asked what this time consisted of, that is, what activities were being performed, and what drove the need to perform the activity. The conclusion from this analysis was that the automotive sector was a relatively undemanding use of sales and technical resources, for the following reasons:

- Orders were not only high volume but also relatively predictable. There was little cost caused by interruptions to other production runs or by the need to purchase or expedite materials unexpectedly.
- The number of customers in the automotive sector was relatively small and the amount of salesman and sales manager time devoted to them was small relative to the amount of business being done with them.
- Marketing activity in the sector was lower than in either of the other key sectors in which the company was active.
- The establishment of long-standing relationships with automotive sector customers had resulted in a low level of demand for technical support from those customers.

The resulting profitability analysis had two key benefits for management. Firstly, it compressed in financial terms the conclusions set out above, thereby providing support for future customer and market focus decisions. Secondly, it enabled management to predict the likely cost implications of any changes in each market segment, for example, the introduction of a major new automotive customer or a move to just-in-time manufacturing by an existing customer.

Output: format and frequency of production

One of the key propositions of this book is that cost management information should only be produced as often as it is useful to management. Another is that information should be produced in accordance with the period of time over which it has influence. Thus, there is certain information that should be produced very regularly: this may be monthly, weekly, daily, or even by the hour. The more immediate the response that management can make to receipt of the information, the more likely it is that it needs to be produced quickly and frequently.

If customer profitability analyses were reported in full and on an actual basis every month, there would almost certainly be short term factors that would distort the results and therefore prejudice management decisions that were taken as a result. The nature of the investment of resource in support of the manufacture of a product, or in the servicing of a customer, is such that the actual resource requirement may fluctuate considerably from one monthly accounting period to the next. Like any other business process, it must be managed over the natural cycle-time of that process, and not to comply with the dictates of financial accounting.

The timing of reporting of profitability is therefore dictated by the way in which the reported information will be used by management. Typically, in practice, customer profitability reports are produced either quarterly or every six months and tie in with budget-setting, strategic reviews and major price negotiation rounds with customers.

Uses of profitability analysis

The periodic reporting of profitability, whether by customer, brand, market segment or any other channel of distribution, has a wide range of uses for management. Traditionally, many businesses have had only the most basic tools to facilitate an understanding of how and where non-factory costs are incurred, and those that have invested time in incorporating profitability analysis into their reporting routine have reaped considerable benefits.

Notwithstanding the example of the engineering components company given above, a conclusion that sometimes emerges is that a high volume customer is shown to be less profitable than had been assumed, or even to be unprofitable. What should the company do? Stop doing business with the customer? Increase prices? Give discounts to encourage customers to place larger orders? Change the way in which it does business with the customer? Any of these approaches **may** be valid. As with many types of management information, profitability analysis often creates more questions than it answers. The important point is, however, that management will be in a better position to understand how resources are being used and whether they could obtain a higher return if they used them differently.

It is interesting at this point to compare product costing with customer costing exercises. Many companies have undertaken an activity-based exercise to look at their product costs and it has been an interesting insight for them. However, their scope to make changes as a result of having more meaningful product costs has not been as great as they would have liked because of the realisation that few indirect costs will change if product volumes or mix is altered especially in the short term (as discussed in Chapter 4) and their scope to change selling prices is limited.

The experience with customer profitability is often different. Here, resource levels (beyond product costs) such as salesmen, marketing spend, delivery costs, telesales and sales order processing can be increased and decreased much more easily than many product-driven costs. Also, customer-driven resources are easier to switch between customers and market segments than product-level costs (where production processes are often only suitable for one type of product). Thus, many companies who start out looking at product costing end up with a customer profitability analysis, and find the exercise to be very worthwhile with significant changes made. Indeed, this can raise an important point about the way the business is managed. The provision of customer profitability information can change the emphasis away from managing by principal reference to **product margin** to managing by principle reference to **customer profitability**. How far this is appropriate will depend on the circumstances of the business.

The importance of customer profitability is further emphasised, for example, by considering those businesses which sell directly to large retailers. The buyers of large retail companies have sophisticated direct product profitability (DPP) systems and a thorough understanding of the impact of supplier arrangements (order frequency, deliver patterns, carton sizes) on their costs as well as a strong desire for keen prices. To be able to negotiate successfully, manufacturing company salesmen must have the same understanding of the impact of customer-driven costs on their cost base.

Life cycle profitability reporting

The importance of reporting information to management to the appropriate level of detail, at the appropriate frequency and with a focus on what the recipient can influence, has already been stressed in this chapter. However, the unwritten assumption so far has been that all such reporting will take place within the context of the annual planning, budgeting and reporting cycle.

Life cycle profitability is, however, an increasingly important aspect of management reporting. It is based on the principle that at several points in the life of a product, customer or contract, important decisions are taken regarding investment, design, marketing and promotion, selling price and so on, and that these decisions, which continue through

Table 5.2 Typical headings for use in a product life cycle profitability model.

Research and development	Materials	Warranty
Design	Direct labour	After-sales service
Planning	Materials handling	Stock obsolescence
Equipment	Set-up	Equipment write-off
Product launch	Inspection	Capital
Marketing	Purchasing	
Product education	Parts administration	

Month	1	2	3	4	5	6	7	8	9	10	
Investment											
Research & Development	500	500	500								
Design	100	100	400								
Planning			200	200	200						
Equipment				1,000	500			500			
Total Investment	600	600	1,100	1,200	700	0	0	500	0	0	
Launch Costs											
Product Launch							100	250	400		
Marketing								100	100	100	
Product Education								75	75	75	
Total Launch Costs	0	0	0	0	0	0	100	425	575	175	
Operating Costs											
Materials								50	50	70	
Direct Labour								10	10	14	
Materials Handling								8	8	11	
Production Handling								9	9	12	
Inspection								9	9	12	
Purchasing								5	5	7	
Parts Administration								5	5	7	
Total Operating Costs	0	0	0	0	0	0	0	95	95	133	1
Total Costs	600	600	1,100	1,200	700	0	100	1,020	670	308	2
Income									100	250	3
Contribution	(600)	(600)	(1,100)	(1,200)	(700)	0	(100)	(1,020)	(570)	(58)	

Figure 5.6 Product life cycle profitability model.

conception, birth, growth, maturity and decline, must all be supported by an understanding of their likely implications over a relevant and appropriate time period rather than over an arbitrary one of twelve months.

Table 5.2 demonstrates the types of heading that would typically appear in the life cycle profitability report of a manufactured product. Its use would begin at the design stage, with the construction of a model based on an understanding of the likely activity profile arising from the requirement to manufacture the product as designed. To this can, of course, be added all the other costs that will be incurred in launching and supporting the product. Against these costs are set projected income. The model can be used both to report historic profitability or, more powerfully, for planning purposes, especially to support investment decisions.

Many costs incurred throughout the product's life will not be discrete to that product, but will be shared resources. It is here that activity-based approaches to life cycle costing can be of use by providing a meaningful way of allocating costs to the product.

12	13	14	15	16	17	18	19	20	21	22	23	24	TOTAL
													1,5000
													6000
													6000
	300						300						2,6000
0	300	0	0	0	0	0	300	0	0	0	0	0	5,300
													7500
50	50	50	50	50	50	50	50	50	50	50	50	50	1,0000
25	25	25											3250
75	75	75	50	50	50	50	50	50	50	50	50	50	2,0750
90	110	110	110	130	140	140	140	155	155	155	155	155	1,9950
18	22	22	22	26	28	28	28	31	31	31	31	31	3990
14	17	17	17	20	21	21	21	23	23	23	23	23	2990
16	19	19	19	23	25	25	25	27	27	27	27	27	3490
16	19	19	19	23	25	25	25	27	27	27	27	27	3490
9	11	11	11	13	14	14	14	16	16	16	16	16	2000
9	11	11	11	13	14	14	14	16	16	16	16	16	2000
71	209	209	209	247	266	266	266	295	295	295	295	295	3,7910
46	584	284	259	297	316	316	616	345	345	345	345	345	11,1660
50	400	400	400	500	550	550	550	550	600	600	600	600	7,300
04	(184)	116	141	203	234	234	(66)	206	256	256	256	256	(3,866)

A life cycle model such as this does depend on predictions concerning activity levels, costs and revenues. However, the need to make such projections is integral to any planning process and should not deter people from the task.

The data entered into the life cycle model can, of course, be translated into annual budgets by cutting a twelve-month segment across the life cycle period. In Figure 5.6 a life cycle model for a period of twenty-four months is illustrated. Such a model has many similarities to a capital project evaluation except that the focus is on a product and not equipment. In Chapter 4 it was suggested that 85% of manufacturing costs are fixed in the design of the product and its process. This reinforces the need to understand the possible impact of the product on the business over its whole life, and not just in accounting periods.

The uses of profitability analysis range from the highly strategic to the operational. Strategic applications include the identification of profitable market segments, customers, customer types and distribution channel, and may help management to take long term decisions about areas that justify either investment or disinvestment. Equally, the reporting of profitability can provide an initial point of enquiry that enables management to unearth operational problems in a specific business process, that may be addressed through organisational or personnel changes, business process redesign or changes in the management of the customer relationship. Finally, customer profitability analysis provides a very sound basis for decision support in price negotiations.

Chapters 4 and 5 have introduced the concepts and uses of product costing and profitability analysis, and have referred in several different ways to the opportunities for improved performance and resource development that may emerge from such analysis. The following four chapters consider the ways in which such opportunities can be exploited.

CHAPTER 6

Budgeting and cost reporting

Annual budgeting is one of the most widely practised disciplines in business. At its best it is a real opportunity for lower and middle management to express their needs and plans for the coming twelve months and for senior management to decide how resources should be allocated in accordance with the business's strategy, priorities and prospects. This chapter discusses how budgeting, in all its forms, can be made more useful.

Although they are essentially concerned with the short term, annual budgets are normally comprehensive financial forecasts. Moreover, they have a particular urgency in that they provide the standard and most public framework against which managers are assessed and judged. It is, therefore, not surprising that budget-setting is taken seriously. That is far from saying, however, that the traditional budgeting model is taken seriously. Often budgets are a means for managers getting what they want. A relaxed budget will secure a relatively easy twelve months, a tight one means that their names will constantly be coming up in the monthly management review meeting. Far better to shift the burden of cost control and financial discipline to someone else. Budgeting is an intensely political exercise conducted with all the sharper managerial skills not taught at business school, such as lobbying and flattering superiors, forced haste, regretted delay, hidden truth, half-truth and lies.

There is no doubt that activity-based approaches can and are significantly improving the quality of budgets, the way actual performance is monitored and, most importantly, the quality of management discussion and understanding of cost behaviour.

It is the purpose of this chapter to describe these techniques particularly with respect to setting manpower and expense budgets. Long range planning and sales forecasting will not be covered, although clearly there are important interactions between these systems and budgeting which will be touched upon.

Traditional expense reporting

The report format shown in Figure 6.1 is almost universal. It shows a comparison of actual versus budget expenditure by expense line item, current month and year-to-date, for a cost centre. Typically such reports are distributed to all cost centre managers between one and four weeks after the month end.

This information does not really help cost centre managers to do their job. It is too late. Usually the main items of expenditure are manpower-related and, by and large, managers know whom they employ. Other costs (e.g. telephone bills) are often rather arbitrarily allocated and furthermore what is reported as actual expenditure is often an accrual made by the accounts department.

These reports need to be understood for what they are, which is to act as part of the internal financial control system ensuring that all items of expenditure have been properly authorised, and to support the build-up of the monthly profit and loss account. The accounts department relies on managers to cry foul if they see something unexpected. Diligent checks can then be made. The traditional reports are a useful way to involve other managers in monitoring financial integrity. They have, however, arguably been pressed into service beyond their design specification as mechanisms for monitoring managerial performance.

In addition, by attributing resources, particularly manpower, to managers this reporting mechanism reinforces an attitude of resource

	Current Month			Year-to-date		
	Actual	**Budget**	**Variance**	**Actual**	**Budget**	**Variance**
Salaries						
Pensions						
. . .						
. . .						
. . .						
Stationery						
Telephone						
Rent & rates						
TOTAL						

Figure 6.1 Traditional expense reporting.

ownership. This itself creates misconceived ideas of self-worth: I have a big budget therefore I am important. Even today, many managers would regard a cut in their budget as a personal defeat and evidence of lost stature, unless possibly all managers had suffered the same fate and to the same extent. Closely associated with these attitudes is the familiar identification of the accounts department with the police department, and perhaps the secret police at that. This is not the way it should be. What is needed is a mechanism for bringing managers together in a more holistic approach to the management and allocation of resources.

The planning/control cycle

There is one further issue that needs to be faced in considering management behaviour before improvements in the budgeting process can be discussed. The theory behind most planning systems (and budgets are simply one manifestation of these) is expressed by the idea that managers formulate clear plans, then action those plans, then measure the consequences, and finally use these measurements to adjust their plans so that the whole cycle can start again. This is represented schematically in Figure 6.2.

The theory of the planning cycle is that of a closed loop control cycle. Plans are adjusted by measuring the effect of our actions. But does this theoretical control loop really happen? Perhaps, but experience and observation show a different behaviour which can be represented by Figure 6.3, representing the planning cycle in practice.

What tends to happen is that managers do what they were always

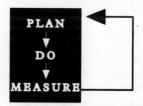

Figure 6.2 Theory of planning systems.

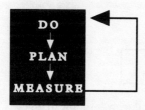

Figure 6.3 The planning cycle in practice.

going to do as a result of inertia ('do what we did last year') or follow their particular agenda and priorities ('I will do what I want to do, which is not necessarily what the business needs'). The plan submitted for approval is at best a post-rationalisation. The point is that the real thinking process that determines management behaviour is not laid bare for critical review in many traditional budgeting exercises. In this syndrome the feedback loop between measured results and action is still present, but in the next stage even this is lost and the situation portrayed in Figure 6.4 results.

The final degradation of the planning cycle occurs when the managers' actions are only weakly connected to the public statement of what is planned. Measurements are related to the stated plans but in practice this is ignored until reality intervenes.

What happens is that measured results are fed back into the planning system and these are discussed with all seriousness by managers, but this is completely disconnected from what managers actually do when they leave the meeting room. Initially the problem may not be too severe, but in time a situation arises where the plan is little more than a dream bearing no relation to reality.

This tendency occurs with varying seriousness in most organisations and the full solution often lies in understanding the relationships between managers and the culture and style of the business. Such matters are perhaps beyond the scope of this book, but the essential point here is that budgets must be firmly connected with activities and this connection must be visible and constantly maintained.

Priority-based budgeting

An early approach to the problem was the concept of priority-based budgeting (PBB), and this is still a valuable and popular technique. It is often used as a one-off cost reduction programme, as well as being

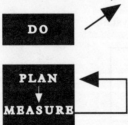

Figure 6.4 Managers probably do what they were going to do anyway.

consolidated into the annual budgeting round. As a process it needs careful and sensitive introduction to managers, but generally wins acceptance because it is manifestly fair and highly participative.

The basic principle behind PBB is to ask managers to identify the activities in their cost centres and then to package these into discrete 'decision packages'. Each decision package is a request for resource, showing:

- A cost, normally both in terms of manpower and money
- A description of what activities will be undertaken with the resource
- A statement of the benefits that will ensue if the activity is funded in the budget
- A statement of the consequences which will occur if the resource is denied

The decision packages are then ranked into a list (the most important activities being at the bottom of the list, the least important at the top). Subsequently senior management can set a funding level at the desired or required level of spending. Thus, decision packages are funded up to the point of the spending limit. Funded packages are given approval while the others are not, or if already ongoing are stopped and the freed resources either redeployed or let go. The idea of ranking projects for capital expenditure approval is common and well accepted. Priority-based budgeting performs the same service for more routine expenditure. The idea is demonstrated diagrammatically in Figure 6.5.

The process is relatively simple. Normally the implementation will take the following steps:

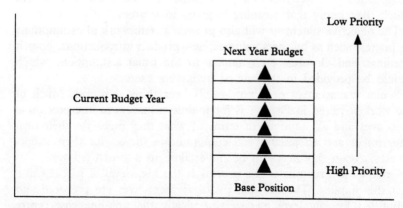

Figure 6.5 Priority-based budgeting.

Phase 1: set-up
- Setting corporate objectives
- Identification of cost centre activities and objectives
- Supplier/receiver reviews

Phase 2: budget preparation
- Preparation of decision packages
- Merging and ranking decision packages
- Funding decision

Phase 3: implementation
- Implementation of actions
- Reporting

These steps are discussed in more detail below.

Phase 1: set-up

As with most things the more thought and effort put into preparation, the better the final result. A PBB exercise works best if it is undertaken within a sound framework of well-communicated corporate objectives. Experience suggests, regrettably, that this is often done poorly in many businesses. A sound way of approaching this issue is to use the balanced scorecard approach described in Chapter 8. This provides not only a statement of strategy and vision but specific objectives for the main issues of customer satisfaction, business process, organisational development and financial results. It is the discussion of these specific objectives that gives the vision meaning. Many vision or mission statements are little more than annunciations of virtue; it is through the detailed examination of objectives and performance measures and the choices which they imply that meaning is given to strategy.

The objective statement will also provide a framework of assumptions on matters such as business volumes, new product introductions, branch openings and closures, etc., similar to the usual assumptions which should be provided in the annual budgeting exercise.

Senior management need not specify everything, however. Much of the work required in Phase 1 is for middle managers to interpret these objectives and assumptions in terms of what they mean for their own department and to discuss and communicate these with their subordinates. Again this needs to be undertaken in a structured way.

One of the strengths of the process is the high level of participation that this implies. The decision packages themselves are prepared and submitted by low level managers, typically the first-line cost centre managers in the organisation. The first step is for these managers to prepare a detailed statement of the activities which are undertaken by their cost centres. Normally this will mean preparing a detailed list of what was done last year complete with activity volumes and man-weeks of effort. From this baseline and in the light of the overall objectives for the next year, the cost centre manager prepares a statement of their own objectives, the activities the cost centre will undertake (including any new ones), and the effort planned and resource required for the coming period.

An important additional element in the discussion of proposed activities and objectives is that it should be conducted in a broader forum than the department itself. Many activities are in the nature of services provided by one cost centre to another. This internal supplier–receiver relationship needs to be explored and the receiver should be given the opportunity to comment on and correct the plans and objectives of the supplier. This concept is considered more fully in the section on service chains later in this chapter. For the moment it is only necessary to observe that the activities and objectives of cost centres should be agreed with receivers.

The set-up phase of a priority-based budgeting programme can be time-consuming, particularly the first time the process is run. However, it does become easier in later years and the wide scope of communication both vertically (through the management line) and horizontally (through supplier–receiver meetings) based on very specific discussions of particular activities provides a firm foundation for the following stages.

Phase 2: budget preparation

During Phase 1 planned activities are identified and costed. Few constraints are built into the process up to this point and managers are encouraged to identify what they would like to do. Now, however, the whole question of cost and benefits must be addressed.

Each cost centre manager is required to review their proposed activities and develop a suite of decision packages each comprising one or more activities. The first decision package, usually referred to as the base package, will contain the fundamental and essential activities undertaken by the cost centre. The problem of course is that managers will quickly assert that everything they do is essential. So to force the issue, an arbitrary rule is invoked stating that the cost of the base package must be say, 70% of the current cost level (a lower figure can be used if thought appropriate). This is tough. It would almost certainly be suboptimal for the cost centre to operate at this level, but this challenge forces the issue and gets managers to question what they really do. It provides a platform from which other decision packages, which typically each equate to about 8% of a cost centre budget, can be constructed.

Creating decision packages requires imagination and careful thought. It is also daunting and for this reason it is essential that a facilitator from outside the manager's department should be available to challenge and help the cost centre manager. In order to create a base package sacrifices will have to be considered such as:

● Cutting out some activities altogether
● Cutting back other activities with consequences on ability to cope at peak times, level of service and so on
● Fundamentally reorganising the way things are done

However, it is also often the case that some activities are clearly not essential and can be given a lower priority than the base package.

Each decision package, including the base, sets out certain header information such as the cost centre involved, and name and number of the package, and the following information:

● The package cost in terms of man-weeks and value
● A description of the activities that will be undertaken
● A statement of the benefits which this package will bring normally linked to performance objectives
● A statement of the consequences that will occur if the package is not funded (limited to statements of fact)

A cost centre manager can bid for more than his existing resources by introducing additional decision packages, although normally only with the consent of senior managers.

Some annotated examples of decision packages are provided in Figures 6.6 and 6.7, and two of the great benefits of this approach to budgeting are immediately apparent:

● The packages give senior management great insight into what is going on in the cost centres concerned.
● The priorities of the cost centre manager are also apparent and, if needs be, can be corrected.

The home economics section of a major utility provided an educational and appliance testing programme in order to create consumer goodwill and confidence (see Figure 6.6). The decision packages provide a simple but clear plan of how the new manager proposed to utilise resources and a statement of priorities and objectives.

In the example of Figure 6.7 the accounts department was required to undertake considerable effort in preparing invoices as well as chasing debts. The decision packages generally show a graduation in service levels for these two services. In this example, Package 2 was really an essential activity but had to be shown separately to comply with the budgeting rules for creating decision packages; this package had an easy time during the ranking process.

At the end of this stage the cost centre manager will have a base package of, say 70% of the costs and four more packages each with approximately 8% of the cost in priority order. The activities in the last package will be the least important, in the view of the cost manager.

Once each cost centre manager has created their own suite of packages, the next step is to get all managers within the same department together and produce a merged ranked list for the department as a whole.

During these ranking meetings all decision packages are reviewed, discussed and challenged by each manager's peers and normally a certain amount of redrafting is called for at the end of the meeting. However, the main task is to obtain consensus amongst the group on the combined ranking of decision packages and it is this list that is taken forward by the departmental manager to the next round of ranking meetings which culminate in a final ranking meeting at director level.

It might be expected that these ranking meetings would result in acrimonious fights. In fact, experience shows this is rarely the case. The lower level meetings are often more objective discussions than subsequent meetings, which may reflect the fact that the decision packages are more similar in nature than occurs later. In an accounts department meeting, for example, most of the packages will relate to accounting, but later discussions will be on the relative merits of an accounts department package and a personnel or marketing package, and the issues require more judgement. For this reason senior managers must be fully involved in the process and committed to it. Considerable care and preparation are required to ensure that the final ranking meeting is conducted in an informed and businesslike way.

The argument is often raised that it is impossible to compare different decision packages from different parts of the organisation, but such arguments duck the issue. The reality is that the business is making such decisions all the time. Budget allocations must always be made and, in resource-constrained circumstances, what one department wins another

Description	Staff	£000	
More exhibitions	–	50	5
Visit additional 200 schools	1	50	4
Revise educational materials	1	90	3
Additional regional materials • coordinate training • consumer database	2	110	2
Major customer services • testing appliances • ideal home and major exhibitions • visit 500 schools p.a. • policy	5	500	1 Base
	9	800	

Figure 6.6 Budget packages for an educational and appliance testing programme.

Description	Staff	£000	
2 day improvement in turnaround 3 day improvement in average outstandings	1	15	4
2 day improvement in turnaround 4 day improvement in average outstandings	1	15	3
Identification of 90% errors 4 day improvement in average outstandings	2	40	2
8 day turnaround on invoicing 48 days average outstandings	6	80	1 Base Package
	10	150	

Figure 6.7 Budget packages for preparing invoices and chasing debts.

loses. The point is that the issues are not normally brought out into the open and considered explicitly. This is the great strength of priority-based budgeting: everyone has an opportunity to join in the debate, the issues and choices are laid bare, and the decisions, once made, are clear to everyone.

The final ranked list is an authoritative document setting out the priorities of the organisation. By accumulating the costs of the decision packages the senior managers can collectively agree on a funding decision, and by examining the decision packages close to the funding line, understand the consequences of that decision.

Phase 3: implementation

The final phase of a priority-based budget is to fund the agreed packages and to take action to eliminate the non-funded ones. Clearly this programme will be specific to each organisation but some general comments may be helpful.

The first point to realise is that this budget is a two-way contract between senior and lower level managers for each decision package. Senior managers can legitimately require that managers deliver what they promised in the funded packages. But by the same token junior managers can point out that unfunded packages have been denied and that they cannot be expected to deliver the activities and services included in these. The point is more serious than it sounds. Many managers have had the experience of seeing their budgets cut, but still being required to produce the same output. In introducing a priority-based budgeting system it is important that the right cultural tone is struck and that the contract is honoured both ways.

The other obvious, but important, point is almost an extension of the first: the budget is a statement both of resources required and activities to be performed. The priority-based system has given managers a budget, but they cannot go and spend it and allocate resources as they see fit. It should be spent carrying out the activities defined as having priority in accordance with the objectives of the business, that is, the funded packages. This is precisely the point made at the beginning of this chapter about how plans can become disassociated from what people actually do.

Of course some latitude is required as with any budgeting process. Managers need to be able to respond to changing circumstances, but normally such changes are marginal compared to the great bulk of day-to-day work undertaken; the link between activities and budgets must be maintained.

Related to this point is the question of what happens when, during the course of the year, new work programmes are identified. In principle the answer is easy: the relevant manager should submit a new decision package for consideration and ranking. In practice this is usually done only when additional resources are required and then perhaps within certain tolerance limits. How to establish such limits is again an issue which depends on the culture of the business and the same applies to the reporting and control mechanisms to ensure that decision packages are being implemented.

Priority-based budgeting is one method of creating a linkage between activities and budgets and it can be very effective to establish real management control over the planning process. Introducing a system of this sort requires commitment and effort. It invariably produces significant cost savings in the first year but the true benefits in control and management focus tend to come later when managers understand the dynamics of the process. It is highly participative and designed as a change management process.

The next sections of this chapter will first review service improvement approaches to budgeting before considering a gentler and perhaps more cerebral approach based on activity matrices.

Service improvement approaches

Quality programmes, quality circles, customer-first programmes and similar concepts have become very popular in recent years. Many of these management philosophies bring with them the idea of local empowerment and the erosion of rather rigid hierarchical management structures in favour of more open networks. The vision is that managers should regard themselves more as 'mini' managing directors responsible for their own cost centre which is now seen more as an internal business or bureau serving other business units within the organisation. Thus the personnel department would be conceived less as a functional leg in a bureaucracy and more as a bureau providing recruitment, counselling, legal and other services to the rest of the organisation. In principle, this service culture should produce a more motivated management and a more adaptive or responsive organisation.

In practice, this style of organisation seems to be some way off, but the ideas behind it are increasingly popular. Certainly senior managers respond to the idea of making people accountable for the services they consume and many organisations have cross-charging mechanisms particularly for IT services. Sometimes these systems are relatively crude allocation systems (e.g. allocating 'group' costs to operating subsidiaries), but they can be fully fledged internal billing systems complete with invoicing, appeal and settlement procedures. The problem with this, of course, is the volume of paperwork generated and the danger of sterile debates over the internal charges generating more heat than light. However, without some kind of customer accountability service departments can become self-serving bureaucracies and the quality programmes introduced with such fervour and expense become degraded.

What is needed is a budgeting system which fosters and promotes the service culture.

In this style of budgeting, overhead cost centres are asked to identify the services they provide for others in the organisation, and to set out for each service a service description, service objectives, and current and forecast costs. Each service must be addressed to an internal customer or sponsor with the appropriate cost allocation.

This information can be fed into a database and sorted so that each internal customer receives a statement of all services provided for it by others within the organisation. Normally these statements are accompanied by a short questionnaire covering topics such as:

- The need for each of them (essential, helpful, unnecessary)
- Quality (precise, excessive, unsatisfactory)
- Objectives (agree with stated objectives, disagree)
- Cost (high, satisfactory, low)

The questionnaires are returned and the information is also fed into the database. The replies are then sorted by internal supplier to form feedback from the internal customers about performance.

In addition, summary reports on each department can be produced for review by senior management, identifying problem services. Senior management can intervene by holding discussion workshops to explore the issues and to develop cost and service improvement action plans. This approach has a number of advantages:

- Managers are forced to present their budgets in terms of outputs (i.e. activities and service levels) rather than inputs (resources).
- They must identify a customer for these outputs, and it is surprising how difficult that can be during the first implementation.
- Not only must a customer be found, but they must accept the service.
- The database provides a comprehensive map of service activities which helps with organisation design and economic modelling.

● The cross-functional challenge and discussion in internal supplier–receiver meetings are an effective mechanism for driving change
and productivity improvements.

The process clearly dovetails well with the ideas of service contracts
which are important elements in many quality programmes. Supplier–receiver meetings can be very productive mechanisms for establishing the value of what a department does as opposed to its cost.
Moreover, if handled properly, they can be an important means of
improving the working relationship between departments.

Of course many activities undertaken by departments are done for the
good of the company as a whole, rather than as services to specific
receivers. These activities can usually be coded to the executive board as
a receiver. Often they are in the nature of policy services, particularly in
very large companies. Typically the board is surprised and alarmed at the
level of such services and the cost. What often happens is that overhead
cost centres undertake considerable work in interpreting, communicating
and monitoring policies and initially try to pass this cost up to the board.
When it is rejected there and must be passed to operating units, the real
value of this effort, or lack of it, quickly becomes apparent.

The service database, as well as providing service evaluation
information, is an important asset in its own right. It provides a map of
who serves whom and of how costs flow within the business. In one large
company which undertook this type of programme there was a central
head office function costing over £200m per annum. The business
had about 35 operating units throughout the United Kingdom. The
inclination of head office cost centres to define their services as if they
serve the executive board has already been alluded to. What was
something of a surprise in this example, was the disinclination of head
office cost centres to view themselves as providing services to the
operating units. Indeed the 'balance of trade' seemed to be in the
opposite direction. The head office cost centres absorbed effort from the
operating units and then spent considerable resources providing services
to each other. This produced a self-sustaining circle of costs around head
office departments and was of considerable concern to the directors of
the company who had been labouring to create a profit centre culture
within the organisation and expected head office to serve the operating
units. The service mapping analysis convinced the board that the
quickest and best solution to the problem was a wholesale transfer of
head office activities to the operating units, with a net reduction of some
2,000 jobs.

One of the ways in which this issue can be presented is to look at
departmental trading accounts. It may seem odd to think of the finance

department as having its own trading account, but Figure 6.8 shows precisely this for the finance department of the example company considered above. The figures are only approximate but are of the correct order of magnitude. The department both supplied and received services. Sometimes there is a circulatory point in this arrangement; for example, the finance department provided services to the human resources department who in turn provided human resources services to finance. However, by travelling round these service loops a balance can be established.

What is interesting about the example is the very large cost incurred elsewhere in the organisation in servicing the finance department. The internal resources of the finance department, its own staff costs primarily, were well known by its managers but the fact that the rest of the organisation spent so much in servicing it came as a surprise. Figure 6.8 shows that only 43% of total cost on this basis was incurred directly in the finance department.

Clearly this kind of system sits well with the supplier–receiver module of a priority-based budgeting programme. It also reinforces internal service agreements, and introduces the idea of service maps as a tool for senior managers to investigate the workings of their organisation.

Both the approaches considered so far are essentially bottom-up budgeting systems, albeit with numerous opportunities for senior managers to intervene, review and direct. They are also effective change management systems. Sometimes, however, a more cerebral approach is

£m	Charged in	Charged out
DIRECT COSTS		
Salaries	6.1	
Other	4.2	
Total	10.3	
RECHARGES		
Executive	–	3.9
External	–	1.0
Operations	6.2	11.2
Commercial	1.6	6.9
Human Resources	0.8	0.6
IT	4.9	0.2
TOTAL DEPARTMENT	23.8	23.6
DIRECT: TOTAL	43%	

Figure 6.8 Direct costs and recharged costs for a finance department.

required: a mechanism whereby senior managers can design and evaluate the organisation. This kind of system is considered next.

Activity matrix approaches

The activity matrix approach is perhaps the most evolved form of budgeting in the sense that it provides a comprehensive financial planning, reporting and performance management system and dovetails well with the activity-based approaches discussed throughout this book. The budgeting and analysis effort involved with activity matrices is usually at a rather higher management level than in approaches discussed earlier, and the activity analysis is less detailed.

The basic building block of the approach is an activity matrix of the sort shown in Table 6.1. This shows a typical activity matrix for a purchasing department. The main activities are shown across the top of the matrix and resource costs are analysed across those activities. Where appropriate, cost driver information or activity volumes are also shown and a unit activity cost calculated. Clearly this approach will be easier to implement in some departments more than others but it is useful, even for a support department such as personnel as shown in Table 6.2. In this example of an activity matrix resource has first been expressed as time spent and is then converted into cost (using different rates for grades).

Table 6.1 Purchasing department activity matrix.

| Resource | Activity | | | | | | | |
	Department-sustaining	Update parts list	Update supplier records	Process orders	Set up new suppliers	Process invoice queries	Agree terms	Total
Salaries								
Wages								
Training								
Travel								
Telephone								
Computer								
Sundry								
Total cost £								
Activity measure	n/a	No. of new parts	No. of suppliers	No. of orders	No. of new suppliers	No. of queries	No. of suppliers	

Table 6.2 Personnel department activity matrix.

Resource	Activity								
	Department-sustaining	Projects	Recruitment	Record keeping	Discipline/ counselling	Job evaluation	Salary negotiation	Social	Total
Man-weeks:									
Grade 1									
Grade 2									
Grade 3									
Managers									
Total									
Employee costs									
Other costs									
Total cost £									
Activity measure	—	—	Recruits	Employees	Cases	Employees	—	Pensioners	
Activity level									
Cost/unit £									

The information in activity matrices is easily collected and presented on PC spreadsheets or by using a simple database. This allows for some simplification in the data collection, for example, by having a table of average cost by grade which allows for the automatic costing of man-weeks of effort.

These very simple devices provide a wealth of opportunities for analysing costs, planning, business process design, project appraisal, costing and performance measurement; these ideas will be discussed below. Before doing so, however, it is worth spending some time considering the definition of activities and the control of the initial data collection.

Building activity matrices

The first step in creating any activity matrix is to agree on a common definition of activities. There is a balance to be struck here because, on the one hand managers should be given the freedom to define activities in the most useful way for them, but on the other hand a common definition provides comparability and a better mechanism for modelling the business later on. A simple example illustrates the point. Many managers spend significant time in meetings, some of which may be to do with product planning. Should this activity be described as 'attending meetings' or 'product planning'? Both approaches have advantages; the important thing is to agree a common approach.

One useful way of obtaining commonality is for senior managers to define a number of main business processes and to demand that all activities should be coded or classified by these business processes. So, for example, procurement may be a main business process and any activity occurring anywhere in the company that falls within the procurement process can be classified as such. These may include:

- Raising purchase requisitions
- Obtaining quotes
- Placing orders
- Receiving goods
- Paying invoices

If the business process definitions are chosen carefully, activity matrices will quickly reveal a horizontal cut through all departments of the cost of these processes, while allowing managers some latitude in defining the precise activities which they undertake.

Experience has shown that two activity classifications are particularly useful:

- Departmental administration: this represents all the costs of simply running the department (e.g. recruiting staff, counselling staff, communication meetings, etc.).
- Projects: sometimes major specific projects should be identified separately and a standard project list prepared. It can also be useful to distinguish between standard (i.e. company-wide) projects and specific projects internal to the department itself.

The reason for including these two types of activity is that when the costs of carrying them out across **all** departments are added up, the results are often very surprising in that so much resource is being used to administer the business and to carry out projects rather than routine work.

Reviewing activity matrices

The first and most obvious use of activity matrices is simply to review the information they provide. Almost certainly when the information is presented for the first time there will be significant surprises. The information that often has the most effect is cost per unit of activity. Managers rarely know the cost of processing an invoice, or preparing a quote, or recruiting a salesman and it is important for them, particularly directors, to become comfortable with these numbers and understand why things cost so much or, more rarely, so little. Often this may require a review of the base information and more accurate estimates. Sometimes, however, it requires a more searching analysis of what actually happens to perform an activity. For example, in one company there was consternation at the high cost of processing purchase invoices. What quickly became apparent was that many of the accounts department clerks, being temporary staff, untrained and lacking a good coding manual, were incorrectly coding as many as 60% of all purchase invoices. These were subsequently rejected by other cost centres. There was consequently a need for recoding (again with a significant error rate). This process gave rise to considerable internal friction (particularly when, after the correct code was entered late, the receiving department found that its costs were now unexpectedly high) and problems with suppliers. This created acrimony and a general sense of frustration in the accounts payable department, and of course the best people tended to leave which meant that more temporary staff were required. Corrective action was needed – new coding procedures.

Activity matrices also provide a basis for classifying and examining costs in novel ways. It is relatively simple to ascribe different flags to activities and then sort them on this basis. The idea of looking at different business processes has already been mentioned but other useful ideas are, for example, to review:

- Negative activities (explained in Chapter 9)
- Value-added and non-value-added activities
- Employee support activities
- Discretionary and non-discretionary activities
- Business-volume-related activities

It is this kind of analysis and questioning which gives managers a rich understanding of cost behaviour. Perhaps just as important is the fact that costs are now so visible; managers have nowhere to hide costs – they all have to be attributed and justified as a part of an activity cost.

Business process redesign

One of the most valuable aspects of activity matrices is the fact that cross-functional business process costs can now be examined more easily.

Traditional budgets and cost reports focus heavily on functional cost centres and it is very difficult to understand the dependencies and interfaces across departmental boundaries. Service improvement approaches are one way of reviewing these issues; activity matrices can provide others.

One effective way of examining business processes is to construct a bill of activities for each business process. The idea of bills of materials for manufactured products is well accepted; a bill of activities is a similar idea, and can be represented diagrammatically as in Figure 6.9. Each activity will show activity volumes and costs, and will usually be prepared from the same activity matrices used to develop budgets. This kind of analysis can be very illuminating and can lead to a radical redesign of how business processes are performed.

There is no hard and fast definition of a business process; it is simply a cross-functional group of related activities that provides a useful output or service recognised by management. Examples might be:

- Purchasing (from requisition to payment of invoice)
- Providing quotations (from customer enquiry to quotation)
- Sales order processing (from order to delivery)
- After-sales service (from telephone call to despatch of engineer)

If activities have been defined so that they are categorised by business process it is easy to see how each activity from each department builds up to produce the full cost of the process. The process cost may be of interest in its own right but activity maps can give important insights into the interdependencies of costs and activities. Simply putting

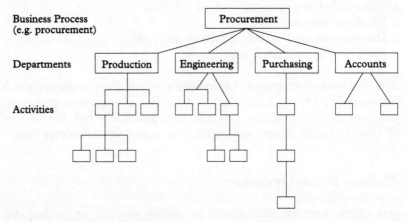

Figure 6.9 Business process design: a bill of activities.

pressure on one cost centre to reduce costs is ineffective and inefficient if the problem lies elsewhere. Moreover, it is only by looking at the business process from beginning to end that sensible planning decisions can be made on how to improve matters. This is true whether in planning performance improvement through more effective working, motivation and supervision, or through investment perhaps in information technology or in redesigning what happens. The subject of process improvement is described more fully in Chapter 9.

Investment appraisal and project analysis

The discussion on business process design naturally leads to IT as a means of automation. IT systems are powerful enablers of change and have dramatically altered many business processes. However, it is also the case that management has been disappointed at the cost savings that many such projects have promised but not delivered.

The problem is a general one: How are cost savings, or indeed increases, which are identified in a project plan then translated into budgets? How can we monitor these savings and ensure they are realised?

Activity matrices help enormously. When a new project is mooted the project sponsor must identify the specific activities throughout the company which will be affected. The cost changes per unit of activity, if applicable, or as a total cost can be identified and built into the project plan. They must also be reflected in the target department's budget.

The debate between the project sponsor and managers responsible for the target activities becomes considerably more real than may otherwise be the case. The managers quickly realise that there is a mechanism in place to ensure that project benefits will be monitored, and that the delivery of those budgets rests with them rather than the project sponsor or IT department. They therefore examine the plans more carefully to ensure that the benefits truly exist.

Budgeting using activity matrices

Traditional budgets are expense analyses presented in a format very similar to Figure 6.1. Activity-based budgets are presented more in the form of activity matrices. Clearly the first step is to produce a baseline set of activity matrices usually based on recent experience, say the last six or twelve months. This needs to be reviewed and examined as discussed above to produce a soundly based document which everybody feels comfortable with as an analysis of current activity costs.

The next step is to prepare a statement of company objectives, and comments and ideas expressed earlier when considering this topic under priority-based budgeting apply equally here. A well-defined set of objectives is a prerequisite to good budgeting, to provide criteria against which resources can be allocated. However, the activity matrices themselves provide a framework for rather more specific objectives. In particular, what is needed is a statement of the individual **activity volumes**. Thus the first step is to prepare relatively high level statements of activity (for example, sales volumes by product class). These are then interpreted by managers in terms of the activity levels in their own departments (e.g. number of sales visits, number of quotations, number of invoices, number of complaints, etc.). This can be thought of as a cascade of information to arrive, at the lowest level, at activity volumes. So, from assumptions about the business environment, come forecasts of product and customer activity, and from these come department plans, and from these come activity volumes. In this way, all budgets are set in accordance with the same set assumptions about the level of business activity.

In their budget submissions managers are required to state explicitly their assumptions about these cascade relationships and this in itself results in a quantum jump in the quality of budget presentation.

Once the activity-level drivers have been agreed, the budgeted activity cost can initially be set at the baseline unit cost times the new volume. Thus, there is now an understanding of the amount of resource required in accordance with the budgeted level of activity. This can be compared with the amount of resource in place, and adjustments made, either up or down, as the budget is set. Once again, this point illustrates the difference between resource consumption (the activity level) and resource provision (the spending that will take place to provide resource).

Not all activities are volume-related and clearly the budgets for these will require a higher level of judgement and explanation. Nevertheless, the comparison from one year to the next provides useful insights into how resources are being deployed. It is important that managers account for **all** their costs in terms of activities. This is important to ensure that there is no leakage of cost information. One of the traditional problems, for example, with assessing the impact of a project on a particular activity, is that a manager may claim that savings on the activity have indeed been realised but a host of other factors have caused the department's costs to increase. The clarity of analysis is lost. If everything is laid bare in a comprehensive activity analysis, however, there are fewer places to hide.

Reporting using activity matrices

The activity matrices are clearly a useful way of compiling budgets, but what about reporting during the year? The ideal solution is to have regular reports in the same format. Unfortunately there are practical problems to this, not least that of data capture. Notwithstanding this, experience shows it is often justified to prepare regular activity reports of the type shown in Figure 6.10, perhaps every six months or even every quarter.

Regular reports comparing actual versus budgeted activity costs provide managers with real insight into how they are using the resources entrusted to them. There are practical problems in collecting information, but experience shows that the best managers do regularly review these issues; poorer performers never have the time.

In order to produce such reports, information has to be collected on activity volumes and actual costs calculated. Clearly this kind of reporting requires more work and data collection than the usual expense reports and the question must be asked whether the benefit justifies the effort. The answer to this will often be yes, provided that there is real senior management commitment to, and involvement in, the process. The reasons can be summarised as follows:

● There is a regular and comprehensive review of how costs are behaving. Initially much of the discussion and understanding turns around refining cost estimates, but eventually managers become firm about these estimates and the discussion then becomes much more centred on the economics of the business and the value of particular activities.
● Management discussion of budgets and actuals becomes far more objective with less scope for political manoeuvring. The management teams become much more focused on the processes within the company rather than the individual departments.
● There is a strong positive correlation between the performance, morale and efficiency of a department, and the understanding that its manager has of how much activities cost and how the department's resources are allocated.
● This reporting format allows specific and real performance targets to be set and monitored by activity.
● Over time (certainly over the first two years) cost levels will often show a significant decline.

One problem often identified with this reporting approach is that resources cannot be put in place to be directly variable with activity

Budget	Department Sustaining	Projects	Recruitment	Records	Discipline/ Counselling	Job Evaluation	Wage Negotiations
Man-months							
Manpower costs							
Other costs							
Total costs							
Activity volume	—	—	Number of recruits	Number of staff	Number of cases	Number of staff	—
Unit cost							

ACTUAL							
Cost							
Volume							
Unit							

Figure 6.10 Activity matrix for the personnel department.

volumes. Resources tend to come in people-sized chunks and do not stay in line with volume movements. However, people can be redeployed, cross-trained and set to remove work backlogs. They can also be transferred from one department to another and back again if necessary. This energetic management of resources is what makes for efficiency and a cost-effective business. Moreover, it is often the trends over several months which are important. This is particularly true in departments where the manning level was established several years ago when demand was at an all-time peak and is now significantly lower.

The main thesis of this chapter is that effective cost control and, therefore, effective planning and budgeting require managers to maintain a clear and firm link between the activities the organisation performs and the resources consumed. Unless there is constant vigilance to make sure people do what they say they will do management control is lost. Traditional budgeting methods and reports are not particularly helpful in this regard. Modern budgeting methods are firmly based on activity analysis and increasingly reporting systems are being developed to support this philosophy. As this is happening the accounts department role is becoming less that of policeman and more one of adviser to managers, helping them manage their resources more effectively.

CHAPTER 7

Operational control

At its simplest, operational control is the process which ensures that what a business actually does is consistent with what it has decided it should do. That is to say, if the strategic planning process decides the destinations, a business plan is the route map and operational control reads the signposts along the way. However, as businesses become more sophisticated, effective operational control must provide the answers to not one but three questions:

- Is the right thing being done?
- Is it being done right?
- Can it be done better?

This means that the signposts which make up operational control should ensure that these questions are continuously asked and answered, and (of fundamental importance) that the necessary adjustments are made quickly if progress is off-course. This chapter will describe how effective operational control can be achieved.

From this simple yet highly relevant analogy for describing operational control the key principles can be derived which will ensure that the control process is effective:

- The signposts (or indicators) must be consistent with the direction in which the business has to go in dimensions such as customer service, product quality and cost.
- The indicators must be read and acted on by the right people within the business.
- The indicators must be presented at the right time in the right way to ensure rapid control and correction.

It is essential, therefore, that operational control is **decentralised**. This is

116

the case whatever the financial management philosophy of the business. Any operational control system which comprises bureaucratic and cumbersome reporting mechanisms will be ineffective because quick reaction is required. The emphasis must **always** be on self-steering and auto-control at the operational level. A centralised approach to operational control, almost by definition, cannot react fast enough or be immediate enough to be effective, because of the time taken for information to be fed to the centre then back again. This does not mean that the centre is excluded from the process, but its role is one of steering and monitoring rather than direct day-to-day involvement.

Many of the concepts described in this chapter were pioneered or developed by Stéphane Doblin,[1] the former chief financial officer of both Fiat and Renault, during his time at those companies. Doblin's approach to operational control is based on four main principles:

- Simplicity of objectives and management information mechanisms
- Coherence of performance indicators with corporate goals
- Future orientation and reforecasting of indicators
- Decentralisation of operational control, both to speed the link between feedback and action, and to engender an entrepreneurial spirit

For example, when Doblin arrived at Renault in the mid-1980s, he found a largely complicated financial reporting structure, with complex reinvoicing procedures between cost centres which resulted in a virtual lack of cost traceability. In addition, there was little focused reporting of non-financial indicators. He immediately cancelled **all** internal recharging, putting in its place monitoring of physical units for intra-company services provided; this considerably simplified the cost structure and significantly enhanced cost control. He also reduced the number of cost centres by 50% in order to simplify cost analysis. The next step was to improve operational control by devolving monitoring and action to individual managers rather than feeding information to the centre and back again. This was achieved by implementing *tableaux de bord* or management control reports locally which focused on fifteen to twenty key indicators. Managers were required to reforecast these indicators constantly in order to improve performance.

This approach provided many of the tools by which the recovery of Renault was achieved.

The framework for operational control

The first principle of operational control is to set the right indicators and measure the right things from the viewpoint of the overall business;

management needs a balanced system to ensure that, if operational managers achieve their goals, then so does the business. 'You get what you measure' is a well-worn saying and there are many examples of how the wrong financial measures can drive a business in the wrong direction; these examples also apply directly to operational control. For example, volume of output as a performance measure may lead to overproduction and excessive stocks. Measuring adherence to the production plan will probably provide much more effective operational control because (on the assumption that the plan is sensible) an overall framework exists. This is consistent with the overall objective of the business to meet customer demand. The volume of production is important and needs to be measured, but it should be treated with care as an indicator for performance measurement.

As an example, a European healthcare business was involved in both manufacturing and retailing consumer goods through an international chain of outlets. In theory, the manufacturing division took orders from the retailers and sold its output to them. In practice, it could sell to them whatever it produced, ordered or not. The key performance measure for the manufacturing division was the internal profit realised on goods produced. Another complicating factor was that piece-work payments formed a substantial part of shopfloor workers' pay. As a result the factory profit was high and material wastage was low; however, finished stocks were high and lead-times to customers were often long. Why? Because the factory manager was more concerned with generating 'profit' than with meeting orders; he made the easy things, and gave the more difficult orders lower priority. In addition, the workforce constantly applied pressure to keep producing as this boosted their pay.

The solution was to measure the factory manager on adherence to plan, lead-time and material usage; whether the factory was full or not was no longer his concern. In addition, piece-work pay was abandoned. As a result, lead-times decreased and stocks decreased as the factory stopped making products which customers did not want.

The key to developing the right framework for operational control is to identify the key operational factors which will ensure the success of the business, and often these factors are clear. For example, in the generic pharmaceutical business a competitive edge is gained by having the goods on the shelf when the customer wants them. If they are not, the customer will go elsewhere because the drugs are not unique to a company but are available from many different sources. As a result, profit margins are usually lower than for research-based pharmaceutical companies. The next key factor is that quality must be of the highest level; any hint of failing to meet regulatory quality standards can be a disaster in the pharmaceutical industry. Finally, in the generic pharmaceutical business price is a key factor in customers' buying decisions, so low cost production is a key factor for success. In this simple example, operational controls relate to one of three headings:

- Customer service
- Quality
- Low cost production

The first step then is to quantify the relevant operational control factors; this should be done clearly and simply.

Customer service

In theory quantifying operational success factors should be straightforward but in practice it can be fraught with 'exceptions'. For example, the customer service level can be defined as 'the percentage of order lines which were filled in full, on the first pass, to the customer's complete satisfaction on the required day'. However, this may appear very rigid in a business which has never had such clear measures. Should the calculation be on number of units, sales revenue or contribution? What if the customer had stocks of the line the company did not fulfil so did not worry about non-delivery? What about the customers who order early because they know the company delivers late? Yet these considerations should not deter management from introducing such measures. The point is that however harsh or unfair it may seem, one simple measure will ensure a clear focus; several complicated measures trying to cater for everyone and every occasion will often only confuse and will provide ample opportunity for bending the rules.

The next step is to identify the functions or activities within the business which influence or determine the particular operational factor. For example, the functions within the customer service chain may be as follows:

- Procurement
- Production planning
- Manufacturing
- Quality control
- Finished goods warehouse (picking and packing)

The third step is to consider **how** these functions or activities contribute to the chain. For example, materials management provides the materials for production; in this sense it is providing an internal service to production and arguably this should form the basis of the main operational performance measure for materials management **for the factor of customer service.** This measure can itself be broken down into its component parts; for example, supplier performance has a considerable impact on the ability of materials management to meet its performance target.

For production, the degree of adherence to the weekly or daily production schedule is likely to be a key measure; however, if the business is seeking to **improve** its service level, it will be important for production to become more flexible so that it can respond to changes in demand. The simplest way of doing this is to measure the trend in production throughput time for major product groups. Again, it is important not to become too complex; it is the **trend** which is being measured, not the pinpoint accuracy of every batch.

In this way, it is possible to identify the operational control measures for each function which are consistent with overall corporate objectives. Figure 7.1 shows an overall framework for this and Figure 7.2 shows the operational control measures that support the defined performance measure relating to customer service. Such measures, depending on how the business is structured, can be summarised hierarchically up to a corporate level, as shown in Figure 7.3.

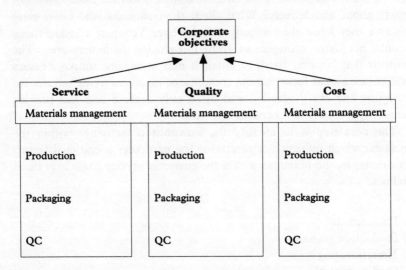

Figure 7.1 Identifying operational control measures for each function.

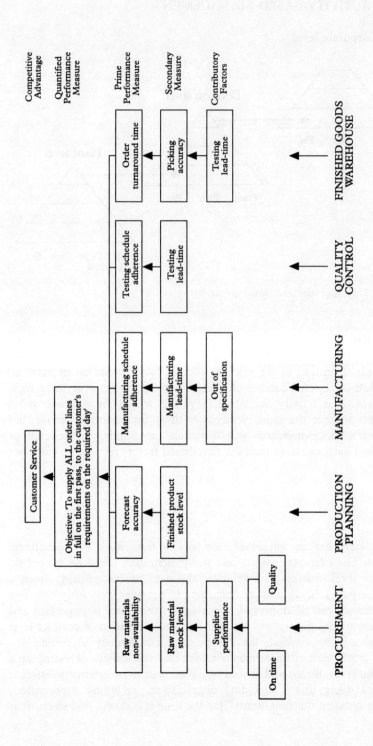

Figure 7.2 Operational control measures for customer service.

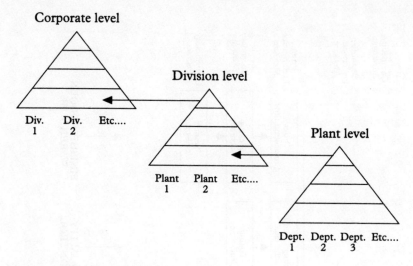

Figure 7.3 Operational control hierarchy.

Quality

A simple definition of the relevant success factor could be to have 'no reworked or rejected batches of product', that is, to get everything right first time. The activity chain to achieve this within the business would probably include the same elements as those for customer service, but the performance measures will focus on the number of rejected or reworked batches rather than the time-based factors relevant to customer service.

Cost

Cost clearly has an important role in any framework for operational control. For example, the success factor definition could be to 'reduce product level unit cost by 5% over the next twelve months'. Such a measure puts a heavy onus on managers to consider constantly how cost performance can be improved. Once again, the **trend** is important and time-consuming discussions about the precise definition of product level costs should be avoided; the key point is **consistency** over time.

For example, a business may consider that the activity of setting up a machine is significant and should be costed, but there are many different ways of doing this – including depreciation, excluding depreciation, using a notional machine 'rental' for the time it is down, and so on. It is far more important to ensure that, whatever the basis, it provides a focus for attention rather than worry what the 'true' costs of set-up are.

It is very important not to become too preoccupied with detail and not to try to identify an indicator to cover every situation; this is quite simply because managers will be unable to assimilate and to act on more than fifteen to twenty indicators. As a result, it is important to consider carefully whether each indicator is really necessary and to exclude those which are just 'nice to know' rather than essential. A possible approach is to select the fifteen to twenty indicators which have the highest priority to begin with and, as performance levels are achieved, to replace them gradually by other indicators; reporting on the original indicators would then be on an exception basis.

Responsibilities

The right framework of operational control measures is of little use unless responsibilities are clearly assigned for each level within the organisation. The fundamental point is obvious but frequently overlooked; it will be dysfunctional and probably demotivating to measure someone's performance on a factor outside of their control. It follows therefore that operational control measures and reporting should be directed at the right level within the organisation (function, plant, division) and aggregated in a logical manner.

To give an example, the performance of the factory manager of a fine china company was measured on capacity utilisation. As a result, he kept the factory full but at the expense of high stocks of unwanted products. Whereas factory capacity utilisation **was** a valid key performance measure at higher levels within the organisation it was invalid for the factory manager. He could only adjust production upwards and had no means of bringing capacity down, if sales demand was not sufficient to fill the plant to meet the target utilisation. Whereas utilisation was a valid measure of the balance between capacity and sales demand, a better measure for the factory manager would have been production schedule adherence and manufacturing lead-times.

In addition, many businesses now realise that it is much better if operational control reflects the way the business works rather than how it is organised (process rather than hierarchy). As a result, for clarity and simplicity of control it is very important to consider whether like functions can and should be grouped together into one 'management centre'; that is to say, whether the organisational structure should be brought into line with the business structure of processes. For example, perhaps separate departments of production planning, purchasing and warehousing should be grouped together into a 'materials management' function because:

- Their activities are highly interconnected and interdependent.
- They have common aims and objectives within the business, i.e. to ensure that production gets the materials it needs when it needs them.

In addition, many businesses are now breaking up central quality departments and devolving them to the functions they service because there are considerable operational benefits. Thus the business would be reflecting the horizontal nature of business processes rather than a vertical functional structure.

It is generally accepted that management reporting according to the traditional functional business organisation is often deficient, for reasons well documented elsewhere in this book. Methods for documenting and evaluating business processes are now well established and in regular use, giving rise to the question of whether businesses should reorganise in order to manage the **process** rather than the functions within it. Some businesses have always done this; for example, in the aerospace industry there may well be a project team to manage a particular order through from design to delivery. In the pharmaceutical industry, some companies see benefits in a team following a drug through the development cycle whilst others do not.

In practice, many organisations opt for a halfway-house whereby managers retain their traditional department responsibilities as a way of controlling staff and resources, but a cross-functional working group of relevant managers meets regularly to discuss and take action relating to the cross-functional processes.

The measures

Another key ingredient for effective operational control is to ensure that managers quickly identify what requires attention; the indicators must be presented at the right time in the right way. Clearly the indicators will be a mixture of financial and non-financial measures. But what should this range of data represent? The best way is to continue the motoring analogy. The report containing the data should be regarded as the dashboard of a car. In France such an operational control report is actually called a *tableau de bord* which translates as dashboard. In English, management control report is probably an appropriate description. This document is the means by which managers can steer the business in the right direction (an example of such a document is given later in Figure 7.5). Management uses the report to support decision-making and to identify quickly the points for attention.

Reforecasting

The nature of the indicators is of course very important; managers should look at actuals versus target, or versus last year or last month, whatever is appropriate. However, there is another key element, which is reforecasting. This means that managers should constantly look **forward** rather than concentrating on the past; historical data should only be used as a basis for focusing on future performance. However, reforecasting should not be confused with just predicting where a particular indicator will be if the *status quo* is maintained; this would be merely a mathematical exercise or, even worse, administering the inevitable. Reforecasting should form the basis of proactive management for the future, where managers are required to explain what **action** they are going to take to bring a particular indicator back into line within a certain timeframe. The benefits of reforecasting in promoting early action are shown, in simple terms, in Figure 7.4.

Many businesses experience considerable difficulties reforecasting financial results four times a year, so it would be clearly unrealistic to expect them to reforecast operational and financial indicators on a weekly or monthly basis, nor is this the point. Essentially, the factors which should be reforecast are those which management can control and for which individuals are responsible. For example, a manager may be unable to control the **volume** of work which goes through their department but they can control its quality. As a result, if the required quality level is 95%, and only 90% is achieved, the manager must explain how they propose to achieve the target level within a period of time. This reforecasting approach provides a very powerful means of formalising a continuous improvement culture into the business.

Timing

Timely reporting of data is the key to management information generally, but nowhere is this more so than in operational control. The timescale depends entirely on the time horizon of related decisions and will obviously vary enormously. For example, consider the reporting of quality data to a shopfloor worker, who will need to know almost batch by batch whether their work meets requirements or requires adjustment. The worker will need to consider these very short term questions:

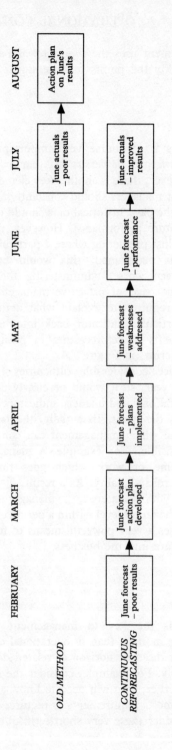

Figure 7.4 Continuous reforecasting.

- Is the machine correctly calibrated?
- Is this batch of materials of the right standard?
- Is the work carried out too slow/too fast?

Reporting this back monthly or even weekly would be useless for operational control; too many problems could have arisen in the meantime. However, the manager of the production department will probably take a longer term view, and weekly or even monthly data may well be appropriate. The manager will need to consider:

- Is the equipment of the right kind?
- Are the suppliers up to standard?
- Is the workforce properly trained?

Robert Kaplan in his conference talks has often used the analogy of ten-pin bowling to highlight the need for fast reporting and feedback. Imagine an operational manager as a ten-pin bowler who has a target for the month of 10,000 points. However, this manager cannot see how many pins are knocked over with each ball as it occurs, but only knows the score after the end of the month. Obviously, this is useless to help with improving technique with each ball because the result is unknown; in addition, by the time the manager does know whether they were successful or not, the circumstances of these attempts would have been forgotten which would make it more difficult to improve. The bowler (or manager) needs rapid feedback after **every** ball in order to meet his targets and to improve continuously.

The concept of the management control report

The management control reporting (MCR) mechanism is at the heart of operational control. With indicators customised to the responsibilities of individual managers and compiled on a timely basis, it is the means by which the business is controlled. It is not just another report, used solely to monitor managers; unless it can be used to **manage** operations, it is almost useless. The key features of the management control report are that it should be:

- Geared towards the future, acting as a focal point for progress towards strategic objectives
- For the operating manager, based on specific financial and physical indicators for each level of control
- A tool to encourage change through self-monitoring and refocusing, so

that senior management can move away from detail and manage strategy.

Three of the key principles of an effective MCR have been covered above (the right indicators to the right people at the right time) but presentation of the report is also a key to its success.

Presentation

The objective of the MCR presentation is to ensure that managers can rapidly and easily assimilate its key messages in order to make effective decisions. As a result, the format should be essentially visual, combining graphics and limited text to enable managers to 'zoom in' on the key issues. The second step is to select the operational control indicators, which is covered above.

The clearest and simplest presentation is to divide the paper in half (or use facing pages) so that, for each section, the recipient is presented with a left side and a right side. The right side should be reserved for the key indicators which the recipient **must** monitor every day, week or month; the left side should provide back-up data to these key indicators so that the recipient can 'zoom in' on particular issues. For example, the right side may contain one indicator which shows the performance of a whole facility; the left side would break down performance by machine. In addition, it is important to include a brief definition of the key factors on the right side; this is a practical point to avoid misunderstandings (accidental or intentional) and confusion over their meaning.

An overview of a typical MCR is set out in Figure 7.5, and a detailed page is set out in Figure 7.6. Operational control mechanisms should and can be implemented rapidly with as little new systems development as possible and maximum reliance on existing data sources. This is because the early implementation of operational control mechanisms will enable operational action plans to be implemented sooner and hence improved performance; it will usually be better to have 75% implemented and running within six months, based on existing sources, than to wait 18 months for 95% following a major systems development. In addition, it is very important to gain management support by producing early successes. The most common reaction when a business is considering the development and implementation of a new operational control mechanism is to agree it is needed, but to consider the data requirements to be enormous. However, it is usually very surprising to discover just how much operational control data actually exists in a factory but which is not focused and reported in the appropriate way. In addition, reasonable

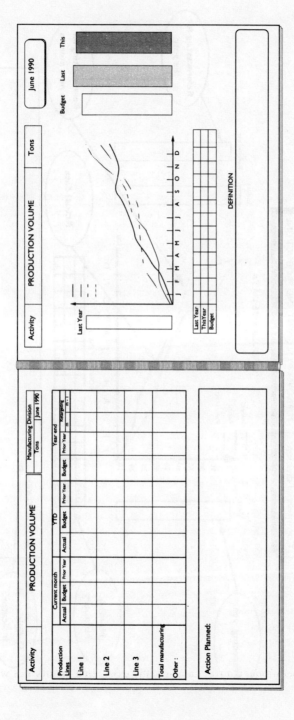

Figure 7.5 Management control reports: format overview.

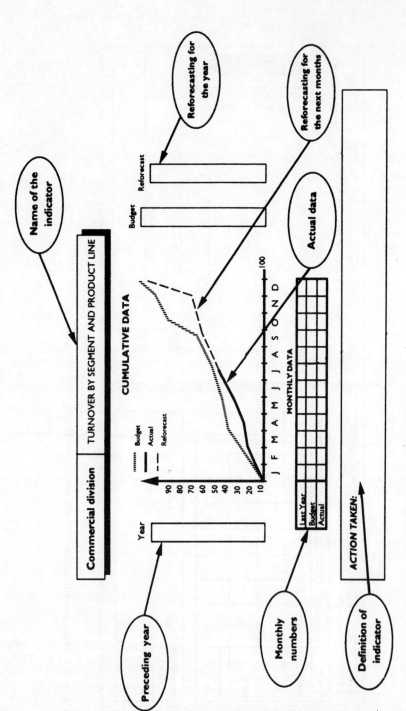

Figure 7.6 Management control reports: detailed format.

approximations can often be made for data which is not immediately available in its specified form. Also MRPII systems can provide a range of data which, often, management never suspected existed.

The basic structure of an operational control system is to use two groups of data sources:

- Physical data, such as cost drivers and transaction volumes, supplied by payroll systems, MRP systems or other systems for specialist functions such as maintenance.
- Financial data, such as activity costs, supplied directly by existing financial ledgers or possibly by PC systems attached to ledgers.

These two sources feed into a system which is, in the first instance, almost certain to be PC-based. An overview of a typical system is set out in Figure 7.7 overleaf.

Link to performance measurement

There is a clear link and overlap between operational control and performance measurement. Indeed, the two cannot be separated. Operational control is principally concerned with doing well what the business decided to do – in operating terms. Performance measurement, as defined here, is concerned with deciding what to do – in accordance with the vision for the business and its strategy. This is described in the next chapter.

Reference

1 S. Doblin and J-L. Ardoin (1989), *Du Rouge au Noir ou les Profits Retrouves*, Public-Union: Paris

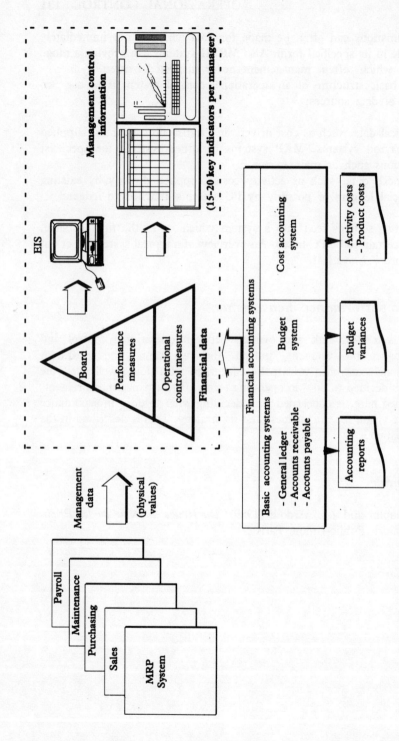

Figure 7.7 Overview of a typical operational control system.

CHAPTER 8

Performance measurement

This chapter examines and explores what performance measurement should mean to boards of directors and senior executives, and hence what information is needed to help in running the businesses. Through the use of a series of models, some of which are now commonly used, a demonstration will be given of how performance measures can be derived and why these should not be primarily internally focused and financial in nature.

The models put forward in this chapter have found widespread acceptance and have helped a rethink of what are relevant performance measures and how they should be presented as management information. This acceptance has often been both at senior management level and, perhaps equally encouragingly, by those tasked with the provision of information to the board. The following areas will be considered in relation to performance measurement as information to senior management:

- The task of strategic management
- The link between strategy and operations
- How the components of board level management information can be determined
- The role and importance of benchmarking in the information set
- The end result – presenting a balanced scorecard

The task of strategic management

The first model used is one that sets out a framework for considering performance measurement at a strategic level and is pertinent to any senior management group. When discussing performance measurement and management information needs with boards of directors, it has been found useful to step back and ask: 'What does strategic management mean to you in your capacity as a board member?' The answers received are highly consistent and can be synthesised into the following:

- Setting the strategic direction of the business
- Implementing and managing the change process in line with the chosen strategic direction
- Improving operational performance of ongoing activities

This can be represented diagrammatically as in Figure 8.1 as three tasks under the umbrella of executive leadership.

Strategic direction

Strategic direction setting, or creating the vision and defining the strategy, is concerned with choosing the right business road and destination. Choosing this road requires a high degree of understanding about the external environment – customers, competitors, demographics, innovation and technology, the likely regulatory environment – as well as an assessment of the internal capabilities or competencies of the company. The potential information volume is vast, so it has to be well analysed and interpreted if it is to be useful in choosing an appropriate strategic direction.

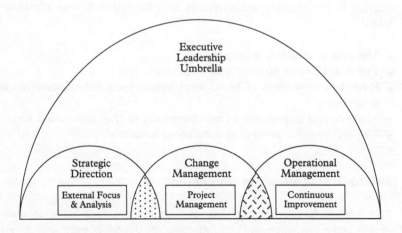

Figure 8.1 Tasks within executive leadership.

Having chosen the strategy (and further discussion of this would be outside the scope of this book), it is appropriate to define the performance measures that will show if the business is still on the right road and how much progress has been made towards the destination. Performance measures are the most visible manifestation of what the business is trying to achieve.

They must be related to what have been identified as factors that will contribute to delivering long term financial success. These are often referred to as:

- Business 'do wells' – the ones that will add consistent long term value to the business in excess of cost.
- Critical success factors: the small number of key factors which are **essential** in the industry if the business is to succeed.
- Order-winning criteria: that is, those factors which **customers** use to choose their supplier, on the basis that focusing on getting these right will give the market what it wants and wins orders.

These will need to be translated or restated in terms of measurable performance indicators. Examples of such performance measures in a manufacturing company could be:

- Market share in defined product-market segments
- Rate of new product introduction (x models per year)
- Product development cycle-time (new product time to market [x months])
- Order-to-delivery cycle-time (process time to market [x days])
- Rating or standing of the company's products in the view of customers

It should be noted that these strategic performance measures are not financial measures such as return on capital employed and profit before tax. Financial measures should be set in relation to the strategic performance goals with financial success being the **result** of delivering the 'do wells'. Financial measures should not themselves be the company's defined strategic performance measures. They are important measures, but alone they are not the ones which will tell directors and management that they are delivering **customer** value and that the company is well placed for its future competitiveness. Many are the companies that have delivered improved return on capital employed (ROCE) and profit before tax (PBT) in the short-run through underinvesting in assets, skills, research and development, only to lose out in the longer term competitive struggle. Winning an annual battle is not a guarantee of winning the longer war. The real task of management is to optimise the value of the business, and not merely to maximise profit in the accounting period.

Change management

Having set the strategic direction and related performance measures, the second task of strategic management is to implement and manage the change necessary to achieve the strategic goals set. Moving from strategic direction to change management is represented in Figure 8.1 by the shaded overlap. This symbolises management's commitment to action – the strategic direction is irrelevant unless there is the will and resources are committed to realise it. The action taken will frequently result in a series of projects, and each of these projects will require their own plans and objectives. Thus, they will also require their own set of performance measures. Take, for example, a strategic objective of achieving a level of market share in a chosen product market. This may necessitate building a new factory and establishing or expanding a distribution network. These projects may take several years and so appropriate milestones need to be set along the way. Milestones such as attainment against time, cost and other resources serve both as performance indicators and as checkpoints against the original project plan. In addition, the validity of the original strategy should be periodically tested. Does it still make sense to be pursuing this particular strategic direction and continuing with this project given, say, a technical innovation which was not envisaged when the project began? What might have made strategic sense two years ago may no longer be relevant.

To summarise at this point, there is a need to monitor progress towards realising strategic objectives using related performance measures and to monitor also the change management process, so directors will require information of a project reporting nature, with each project having clear milestones, performance measures and review points.

Change management projects need not only be tangible in nature. Company chairmen often proudly proclaim 'our employees are our greatest asset', yet often only lip service is paid to enabling this asset to help deliver improvement. Especially in service industries human resource projects, such as skills training, job rotation and changed recruitment profiles, will be as important (if not more so) than tangible asset projects.

It should be remembered that there is an external element to this too. Competitors may have embarked on similar, or retaliatory, strategies. Management should be concerned not only with monitoring their own company's change management projects' progress but also their competitors' actions.

Continuous improvement

The third task of strategic management is that of improving operational effectiveness. One of the most perilous conditions for a business is that of organisational and operational complacency – the belief either that there is little that can be done to improve operations, or that because the company is already the industry leader, in the vanguard of innovation or cost containment, it will continue to be so indefinitely. Schumpeter[1] was one of the first writers to point out that where competitive advantage allows monopoly profits to be earned (returns above normal ROCE) it is only a matter of time before technical and organisational innovation will replace one form of competitive advantage with another – his 'gales of creative destruction' wreaking havoc with the existing economic order. Much of Japanese innovation occurs as a result of many minor innovations and enhancements which cumulatively amount to major innovation. Such a process of creeping improvement avoids the high cost of the search for the (often) unattainable quantum leap in technological advancement, but it is also low risk because changing technologies can be incorporated incrementally.

So, as well as choosing the strategic direction and instigating change management projects, managers must ensure that there is continuous improvement in each and every operational and functional area of the business. The concept is widely recognised and practised in Japanese companies where it is known as 'kaizen'. Using techniques such as fishbone analysis, each work group strives to improve the activities it performs – to lower waste, improve reliability, speed up throughput, etc. This technique can be applied to both manufacturing and service companies. Figure 8.2 shows how fishbone analysis (otherwise known as the Ishikawa or cause and effect diagram) was applied to an airline.

A key cause of falling returns in the airline was found to be its poor punctuality record. This was both a major cost driver, in terms of overtime, crew-out-of-hours, extra meals, hotels and transport, passenger transfer to other airlines, and a perceived cause of deteriorating yields. Business class passengers were reluctant to risk flying with the airline for fear of missing meetings or onwards connections. Taking the Ishikawa diagram down to the next stage where the objective becomes 'improve punctuality' the same process can be repeated, identifying in each part of the business the effect and its cause (Figure 8.3). Having identified the causes, project-based task forces can be pulled together to devise ways in

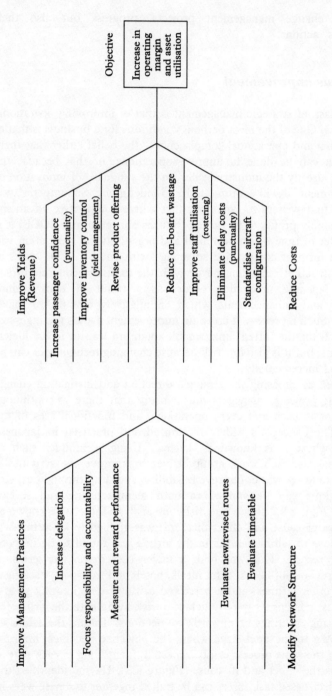

Figure 8.2 Application of fishbone analysis to an airline.

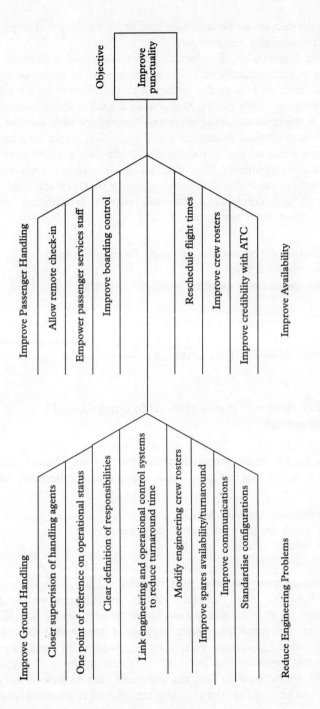

Figure 8.3 Applying Ishikawa to improving punctuality.

which the causes can be eliminated, or at least substantial improvements made to minimise their effects.

These projects, if of sufficient importance, will constitute strategic change management projects. For example, if to be punctual is a critical success factor and the airline wishes to be perceived to be a leader in this area, the punctuality project will assume a level of importance that takes it out of the continuous improvement hemisphere back into the strategic change management hemisphere of Figure 8.1. Other smaller projects will form a natural part of the ongoing continuous improvement process.

Senior management must take an active part in such continuous improvement processes if they are going to be taken seriously by other managers and employees. This will require determining where the greatest need is in terms of:

- Perception of customers' demands for improvement
- Competitors' actions
- The organisation's position relative to competitors

and then translating these into operational or functional objectives for managers. These objectives can in turn be translated into continuous improvement tasks at an operating level.

Linking strategic management to operational management

The tasks of strategic management direction setting, change management and continuous improvement, have significant implications for:

- Performance measurement
- The provision of management information
- The reward system

The truism 'you get what you measure' means that directors must determine what the strategic, change management and continuous improvement performance measures are to be, develop an information gathering and reporting system capable of monitoring these measures and then align the rewards offered by the company to these measures. Of course the measures are not cast in tablets of stone. They will vary widely from business to business and from time to time. The important point is to be sure that the measurement system emphasises what are the important measures so that behaviour is modified and directed towards what is important for the business.

The means by which strategic management becomes linked to operational management, and is communicated throughout the organisation, should be through the business planning process as shown in Figure 8.4. This is then supported by the management information system, which will permit management to judge whether or not the strategic objectives are being met. It has already been suggested that the board of directors' management information should not be considered to be purely the monthly financial 'board pack', resplendent with its complete balance sheet, profit and loss account, and budget variance commentary. In contrast the board pack should report on all of the tasks of strategic management – to recap, these are:

● Strategic direction
● Change management
● Continuous improvement

The tendency to focus on internal financial measures was supported by the findings of a Harris Research study[2] which highlighted a definite introspective orientation by directors of major UK companies. Strategic planners expressed dissatisfaction with the quality of information they had to formulate strategy and with which to monitor ongoing performance against a chosen strategy. Not unnaturally, perhaps, finance directors were more satisfied with the information they received. This no doubt reflected the fact that they tend to have a financial orientation rather than a market one. In addition, being for the most part both the custodian and purveyor of the performance measurement system, it is not surprising that it should reflect their needs and orientation. This orientation is portrayed as a traditional management information system (MIS) (Figure 8.5) in which performance is presented primarily around the statutory reporting unit for financial accounting purposes.

The major problem with this orientation is that it reinforces the view that accounting measures are the only relevant performance measures. Recognising the limitations of pure accounting performance measures by statutory reporting units and the need to consider directional change management and operational measures, a revised picture of a strategic information and measurement system emerges.

In the picture of the information system of Figure 8.6 the external information has two primary elements. The first relates to the socioeconomic environment in which the organisation is operating, the 'macro' scene, which will provide the backdrop to strategy formulation and direction setting. The second element relates particularly to the competitive environment – how the company is doing *vis-à-vis* its chosen

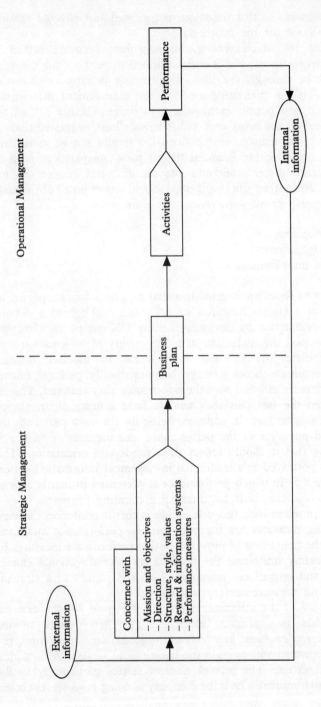

Figure 8.4 The link between strategic management and operational management.

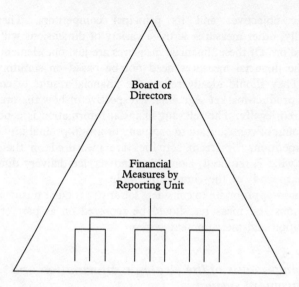

Figure 8.5 Financially orientated MIS.

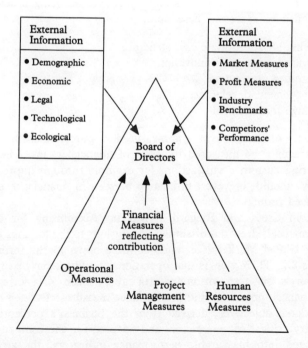

Figure 8.6 Strategic information system.

strategic objectives and its principal competitors. Then, turning internally, other measures across a variety of dimensions will need to be reported on. Of these, financial measures are just one element. However, even the financial measures need not be based on statutory reporting units. They should ideally reflect the financial results of competing in chosen product-market segments, irrespective of how the organisation is structured legally. The relevant financial information is concerned with the amount of contribution to company or group profitability at the point of competition. Upstream activities are measured on their ability to deliver what is required, along cost and service delivery dimensions, to the 'sharp end' of the competitive fight.

It is now appropriate to consider, for any particular business, just what dimensions and measures should be reported on as part of a strategic information and measurement system.

The components of the strategic information and measurement system

In the 1990 conference Winning in the Global Marketplace[3] five factors were stated consistently by senior executives as being crucial for long term business success. These were:

- Having an appropriate cost structure
- Service quality and innovation
- Customer satisfaction
- Management development
- Change management

One only of these – cost – is measured in purely financial terms. The others cannot be measured in terms of financial ratios. The **results** of delivering customer satisfaction, for example through improved service quality, should, however, ultimately be seen in financial terms through enhanced profit.

Kelvin Cross and Richard Lynch in 'Accounting for competitive performance'[4] drew not dissimilar conclusions to the findings in Winning in the Global Marketplace, and set these down in the form shown in Figure 8.7. Their view is that operational activities can be linked to the company's long term vision and strategy by means of a series of market and financial objectives and performance measures. Defined market and operational objectives, derived from the business's perceptions of the industry critical success factors and adapted for the company, must be translated into measurable performance indicators, the attainment of which should deliver a desired financial result.

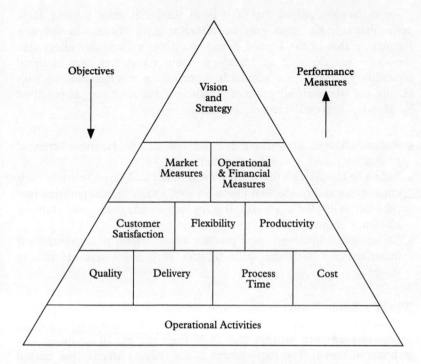

Figure 8.7 Relating operational activities to a company's vision and strategy. Adapted from Kelvin Cross and Richard Lynch (1989), Accounting for competitive performance, *Journal of Cost Management*, vol. 3, no. 1, pp. 20–8.

The key to using a model such as this successfully is to:

• Identify the critical success factors
• Establish relevant performance measures
• Generate the organisational capability to deliver

An example from the car industry to illustrate these three steps was the cementing of Rover's link to Honda. The minimum conditions and standards for market success in the motor industry are now being set by the Japanese. These comprise measures such as mean time between failure (MTBF), reliability as expressed by warranty periods, value for money (VFM) in relation to specification, rate of new model introduction and new model development lead-time. World-class manufacturing standards are being set for labour productivity, skills and flexibility, throughput time, in-bound and schedule adherence time, component reliability, design for manufacture, process simplification, etc.

Rover has recognised that if it is to survive it must achieve these performance levels or at least be within striking distance of the new Japanese plants in the United Kingdom. Rover's directors believe that the only feasible way to transform their company's organisational capability to reach these standards is through a strategic alliance with Honda and wholesale adoption of world-class manufacturing as practised by Honda. This will involve, *inter alia*:

- Radical changes in working practices to achieve Japanese levels of productivity and operating flexibility
- Access to Honda's plants in the United States and Japan to study their engineering and production processes with a view to incorporating best practice at Rover's plants, thereby accelerating its own rate of efficiency improvement
- Collaboration in design, new product development, procurement and manufacturing with the skills transfer very much from Honda to Rover

What the Rover–Honda example demonstrates clearly is that competitive performance requires a refocus of management information towards factors **relevant for success** and away from the manifestation of that in financial terms. The requirement is not only to identify the critical success factors (CSF) and define the performance measures along a variety of dimensions but also to determine how these measures can be achieved. Performance measures are behavioural, and people will respond to what is being measured, but the standards being set must be believed to be attainable. If not, the information reporting system, if perpetually showing under attainment, will merely serve to demotivate all concerned.

Using the value chain: a technique for determining the components of a strategic information and measurement system

Michael Porter's value chain has become widely used as a technique for analysing the value-creating activities of a business. Although traditionally used in a manufacturing environment, an example taken from a holiday tour operator shows how the technique can be adapted for any business (Figure 8.8). It requires thinking about what the key value and/ or cost adding activities are in an organisation's process flow, from suppliers through to the organisation to the end consumer.

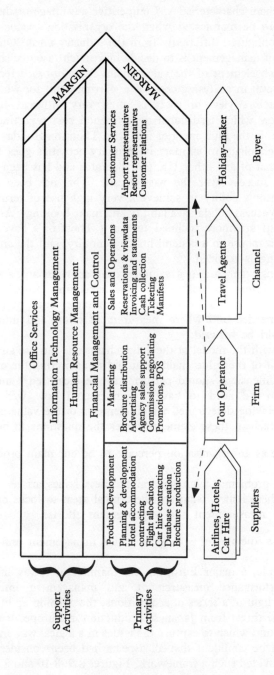

Figure 8.8 Value chain for a tour operator.

In general, organisations operating in the same industry tend to share similar value chain characteristics. Competitive advantage or disadvantage will tend to be manifested when the organisation's value-creating activities are configured differently from the industry norm. One of the primary tasks of management is to decide how much resource should be allocated to each element of the value chain. Activity-based techniques can be very useful in analysing costs as a starting point for which costs fall where. Such a view of costs is often very different from the hierarchical view which traditional departmental cost reporting gives.

For example, in the tour operator industry, Thomson Holiday's use of information technology to support its primary activities goes substantially beyond that of any other UK tour operator and has been a major reason for its success over the past decade. This has been attained through Thomson's ability to achieve a very high use of terminals in travel agents to access holiday availability and make bookings. As a result travel sales staff are more inclined to see if Thomson's have holiday availability in response to a general holiday enquiry, and the amount of paper processing is reduced.

Understanding where the real value-creating activities are, and where the business differs in cost and value structures from principal competitors, provides the basis for determining what performance measures are needed and where measurement effort and information reporting should be focused.

Continuing with the model of the value chain, one can use an analysis of each element of the value chain as an aid to answering the questions 'Along what dimensions should performance be measured?' and 'What information do we need to have to understand how well we are performing?' Having determined which elements of the value chain are most critical, each of these elements forces the questions to be asked:

- What do we as an organisation perceive to be our main problems in this area?
- From these problems, what general business issues arise?
- Related to these issues, what are the critical areas to focus on in our performance measurement and improvement efforts?

Knowing these dictates the basis for the management information system.

As an example, a major European car manufacturer was anxious to revisit its performance measurement and management information systems in the light of a series of acquisitions, the opening up of Eastern Europe and the threat from Japanese production in Europe. It sought a framework around which to capture the issues in a logical way and one in which it could be confident that all aspects had been considered. The value chain provided such a framework. Figures 8.9, 8.10 and 8.11 show

Perceived Problems

- Rising costs of technology
- Product life cycle shortening
- Incomplete CAD/CAM/CIM integration
- Information not seen as a shared resource across the group

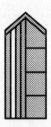

Business Issues

- How does the company avoid duplication of technological development effort in diverse units?
- How does the company stay abreast of competitors' developments?
- How does the company capture learning in one part of the group and transfer it to others?
- How to speed up time-to-market and cycle-time?

Performance Measurement and Information Issues

- Improved project reporting
- Networking at operational level across the group
- Benchmarking new product development cycle-time and competitor innovations
- Dissemination of key technology developments to relevant employees

Figure 8.9 Applying the three-step approach to technological development.

Perceived Problems

- Inability of all units to move to JIT production

- Incomplete adoption of EDI

- Unacceptable quality from suppliers

Business Issues

- Excessive inventory

- Standardisation of components

- Poor quality control

- Coordination with suppliers

- Coodination with other group factories

- Group communications capability vital

Performance Measurement and Information Issues

- Need for: progress reporting on improvement projects

- Inter-unit comparisons (intra-group benchmarking)

- Performance measures applied to incoming quality

Figure 8.10 The three-step approach for in-bound logistics.

Perceived Problems

- Centre unable to compare relative performance of units
- Inability to focus production on plants that enable lowest total cost achievement
- Inconsistent definitions and performance measures across manufacturing units
- Inappropriate reward mechanisms

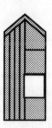

Business Issues

- Worldwide manufacturing costs higher than competitors'
- Fixed cost base higher per unit than smaller local competitors
- How to reduce fixed cost base
- Choice of site for expansion
- Process improvements developed in one area are not transferred/made available to other units
- How to shift manufacture as exchange rates move
- Group communications capability required

Performance Measurement and Information Issues

- Need for standardisation of definitions and performance measures across all units so as to understand relative costs and performance
- Incentives to encourage improvements in group performance, not just unit performance

Figure 8.11 Operations assessed using the three-step approach.

how three elements from the value chain were assessed using the three-step approach of perceived problems, business issues and performance measurement issues for each.

This approach enabled the group finance director to see performance measurement and management information in a new light; namely, one which demonstrated that producing periodic financial statements to the board was only a small part of the picture. It further highlighted how, as the director responsible for the provision of information to the board, he needed to embrace a new vision of what management information meant, or run the risk of losing his power base as others began to satisfy board members' needs for better information.

Benchmarking: an emerging component of information and measurement systems

At various points in this chapter the issue of benchmarking and standards setting has been raised. This is because it has become abundantly clear over the past decade that few companies can now afford the luxury of considering themselves isolated from understanding and learning from other businesses. But what has changed fundamentally from even ten years ago, is that the competition can come from anywhere in the world – cars from Korea, Japan or Malaysia, fruit from Chile, strawberries from Israel, flowers from Colombia. Speed, frequency and cheapness of airfreight enable a vast array of products and produce to be shipped anywhere in the world, providing effective competition to local or domestic suppliers. Advances in IT and telecommunications have enabled research, support and administrative functions to be located anywhere on the globe. Clerical functions, an increasing proportion of some businesses' total cost structures, need not be located at head office in the capital city centre paying prime rents and high salaries. They can be located in rural surroundings, lower cost cities or even abroad. Swiss Air has decided to relocate its accounts function to India to provide a lower cost service to the airline. Already equipped with the tele-communications infrastructure, the function has been 'footloose'. Software development houses are doing the same, using the combination of highly skilled low cost labour equipped with IT links to supply their customers in industrialised first-world economies with sophisticated software.

The significance of all of this is that every organisation needs to be continually alive to the relative performance – efficiency and effectiveness – of its operations and activities against its key competitors and the 'best-in-class' for the functions it performs. If it gets too far out of line (the wrong way) it becomes dangerously exposed. It will begin to lose its ability to compete in terms of product or service offering, or will trade at an uneconomic price, therefore, over time, losing the margins necessary to support its investments in upgrading its facilities or in new products. Every company has to be aware of the industry standards, and benchmark itself against these as a way of understanding its relative position and competitiveness. If the company is performing below the industry norm, it has an immediate reference point for improvement. If it is the industry leader, the 'best-in-industry' setting the standard, as say Toyota is in the car industry for order cycle-time and product warranty, it still needs to track its position against its competitors but should also be seeking to redefine the norm by looking for 'best-in-class' or 'best-in-process'. This requires looking beyond the confines of the industry sector, asking in what other sectors similar processes are performed, which organisations perform these processes well, and then learn from these organisations, thereby setting new norms within its own sector.

The British Post Office, desirous to improve service standards and to become a total quality organisation, undertook exactly this exercise, benchmarking along the dimension of total quality in every activity and process it could. Within Europe the Post Office's standards of delivery performance were already high when compared with other national postal services, but, with the threat of competing services from other businesses (fax, courier services, etc.), it believed there had to be further scope for service improvement. It continues to compare its performance against other postal services but seeks to benchmark itself against other companies in terms of best-in-class or best-in-process with these companies providing the target standard to aim for. Along the dimension of total quality it looked to winners of the Malcolm Baldrige Award as companies from which to learn. These included Motorola, Westinghouse, IBM and Milliken. Clearly none of these competes against the Post Office, but the Post Office sought to take the standards set by these companies along the dimensions of:

- Leadership
- Information and analysis
- Planning
- Human resource utilisation
- Quality assurance of services
- Quality results
- Customer satisfaction

to become a total quality organisation. Its objective was to benchmark its own 'customer-first' process with the achievements of some of the world's acknowledged best-in-process organisations. It sought to measure its process performance against the best. The information it obtained as a result of the exercise formed the basis for its change management projects and continuous improvement targets. These will be actively monitored by senior executives in the organisation.

Benchmarking against key competitors is often easy in terms of the end product and output performance measures, because details of these may be readily available from product literature, industry association statistics or the trade press, or from reverse engineering of the products. Process performance measures are more difficult to benchmark against key competitors. They are less readily obtainable and so have been a major reason for the increasing trend towards two forms of benchmarking. These are:

- Intra-group benchmarking, by which similar units within a group of companies compare process performance, benchmark against each other and set up improvement task forces at an operational level so that best practice can be transferred from one part of the group to another, capturing learning and best practice that has been developed within the group. The centre may be able to provide considerable value by setting the measurement framework by which units can readily compare performance and know that like is being compared with like.

- Inter-industry benchmarking, as done by the Post Office, whereby best process practice is identified in a non-competing business, which cooperates in the exercise. Why should any company be willing to offer itself as the subject of a benchmarking study, so that others learn at its expense? The answer is that the company which is to be benchmarked can benefit from the chance to learn from the 'naive' questions being asked by the visiting organisation. These might spark off ideas for further improvement based on particular practices which might have a relevance for the host organisation.

Benchmarking ensures that the organisation maintains an external focus on best practice, rather than the all-too-frequent practice of basing targets on improvements over the previous year.

If benchmarking in terms of product performance characteristics and process improvement targets is a crucial part of an organisation's strategic measurement and information set, how should companies go about the process? Figure 8.12 sets out the main steps in benchmarking,

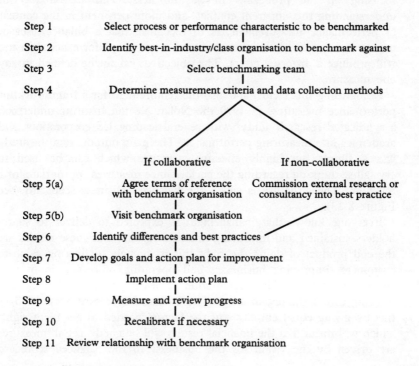

Step 1	Select process or performance characteristic to be benchmarked
Step 2	Identify best-in-industry/class organisation to benchmark against
Step 3	Select benchmarking team
Step 4	Determine measurement criteria and data collection methods

	If collaborative	If non-collaborative
Step 5(a)	Agree terms of reference with benchmark organisation	Commission external research or consultancy into best practice
Step 5(b)	Visit benchmark organisation
Step 6	Identify differences and best practices
Step 7	Develop goals and action plan for improvement
Step 8	Implement action plan
Step 9	Measure and review progress
Step 10	Recalibrate if necessary
Step 11	Review relationship with benchmark organisation

Figure 8.12 The benchmarking process.

distinguishing between benchmarking that is undertaken collaboratively (intra-organisation or best-in-class) and that which is unlikely to be able to be done collaboratively (best-in-industry).

The balanced business scorecard

Faced with the requirement to redefine performance measures, many businesses struggle to cope with what appear to be conflicting forces and to capture their ideas in a structured and cohesive framework. The conflict arises because, for example, *prima facie* some aspects of high levels of customer service do not fit immediately with objectives such as being a low cost producer. There are two ways of understanding this apparent conflict.

Firstly, the aim should be to define what is important for the business (for example, aspects of customer service) and then deliver these factors in the most effective and low cost manner. This will typically require focusing on the **processes** in the business. The second way of understanding this apparent conflict, and more pertinent in the context of performance measurement, is to recognise that a **balanced** set of measures is required. Overemphasis on any one performance measure will produce a distorted effect. The objectives cannot be defined in any one measure.

Recognising this factor, and also the requirement for a **framework** for performance measures, in 1990 the Nolan Norton Institute undertook a syndicated research study[5] with several leading US corporations and academics into measuring performance. The main output from the study was a simple but highly effective structure which can be used to crystallise thinking regarding the performance measures appropriate for a business. The structure is called the balanced business scorecard (see Figure 8.13).

Everyone knows that management is expected to deliver to shareholders sustained and improving financial results. But these results are the end product of doing the right things, namely, delivering value to customers, improving businesses and operating processes, innovating constantly, enabling the organisation to learn and then sharing that learning across the organisation. The balanced scorecard acknowledges this by giving equal emphasis to the factors needed to get them right, which will mean that the financial results will be good. Yet all measures are driven by the vision for the business. In the balanced scorecard

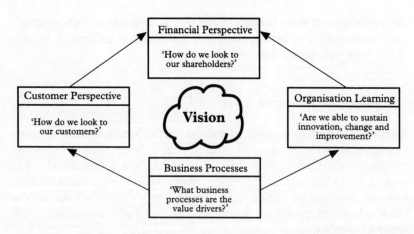

Figure 8.13 Balanced business scorecard. (© Copyright Nolan, Norton & Co. All Rights Reserved.)

management is required to consider and agree the top three to five performance measures in each box. An example of a set of measures is given in Figure 8.14.

There are, of course, no predetermined or industry-specific sets of measures to fit into such a structure. Each business must decide what is important to measure, at that point in time, in accordance with the issues being faced and its vision and strategy. It is for this reason that performance measures are so important. They are the visible manifestation of what is important to the business, and as such are a strong signal to its managers and all employees. Because of this, they are a key tool in influencing **behaviour** such that change is achieved towards meeting strategic objectives. In the right environment, managers and staff will work towards achieving the performance measures set up for the business. The problem with traditional financial performance measures is that it is often hard for managers and staff to see how what they do contributes directly to the whole picture of achieving success in financial terms.

This is not the case, however, with using a structure such as the balanced scorecard. Here, the everyday factors to which everyone can relate are set out in a clear structured manner. In answer to the question: 'What can we do to help improve financial performance?', the answer is to work towards delivering improvements in the measures set out in the scorecard.

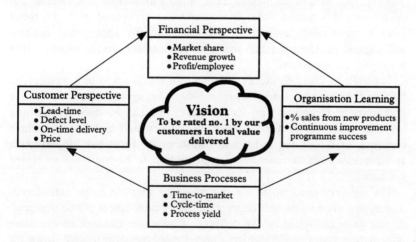

Figure 8.14 Balanced business scorecard: typical performance measures. (© Copyright 1990 Nolan, Norton & Co. All Rights Reserved.)

The structure forms an ideal starting point for initiatives based around performance measures. The first step is always to ensure that strategic objectives are clearly understood and articulated. From this, management can define what it needs to **do well**, to achieve success. From these **do wells** a set of balanced performance measures can be created to suit the structure. This is typically achieved by:

- Senior management brainstorming the key measures for each box and agreeing a balanced set of measures
- Current performance being assessed for each measure and also a target to achieve in a defined timescale
- Rolling out the approach, and requiring managers and project to take **action** to effect improvements
- The new measures becoming a part of regular management information reporting

Measures and targets are then constantly monitored and updated. As has been stressed earlier, the important point with such measures is the **trend in improvement** over time (and not particularly concerned with accounting periods). Some measures will be absolute values such as delivery lead-time in a number of days. Other measures may only be useful in relative terms. For example, an increasing number of businesses carry out customer satisfaction surveys. The results of such surveys may be an important measure in the **customer perspective** box. The fact that 85% of customers are satisfied with service is of interest but on its own this means little. It is only when compared with the **trend** from surveys taken at regular intervals (and the appropriate interval will depend on the business) that management can decide whether it is achieving its objective.

Typically, a set of measures is defined for the business as a whole. The balanced scorecard lends itself to then being cascaded down the organisation. Depending on its structure, this can be done by creating lower level scorecards for the business units, which make up the whole business, or by setting individual measures for functions, departments and processes which represent a contribution to higher level scorecard measures.

The delivery mechanism for the measures also has to be considered. The appropriate route will depend on the circumstances of the business. At one extreme would be the delivery of measures through an executive information system (EIS) which allowed managers also to **drill down** for further analysis into the operating systems that supported the provision of the scorecard measures. The other extreme would be a simple paper-based procedure with monthly updates. The important point here is that

the message is more important than the medium. The circulation of the scorecard measures has to be considered. Confidentiality and sensitivity may inhibit some measures from being widely circulated within the organisation. Beyond such restrictions, regularly publicising the scorecard measures on factory wall charts, staff noticeboards and newsletters can be an extremely effective means of transmitting what is important to the business and engendering a feeling of striving towards common goals.

This chapter has sought to set out some of the more recent thinking on management information for senior executives by combining the results of research, academic thinking and best practice adopted by leading companies. The overriding message is that many businesses need to take a fresh look at what performance means, how it should be measured and what information they should be asking for. The information they receive should enable them to determine where they need to go, what objectives they should be setting and how they will know whether or not they are on track towards their chosen destination. The orientation of the information set will be increasingly outward-looking, covering the macro environment, market measures, competitor performance and standards through benchmarking, and not just a mass of detailed financials.

A system that emphasises the value-creating dimensions of business, rather than just the financial results of these, will ensure that directors focus their attention on their prime tasks:

- Setting the right strategic direction
- Instituting change management projects to deliver what customers value
- Ensuring continuous improvement in business processes and the ability of the organisation to learn

References

1 J. Schumpeter (1942), *Capitalism, Socialism and Democracy*, Allen & Unwin: London
2 The Harris Research Centre (1990), *Information for Strategic Management: A Study of Leading Companies*, Manchester
3 Business International/KPMG Management Consulting (1990), *Winning in the Global Marketplace*, Chief Financial Officers Conference
4 K. Cross and R. Lynch (1989), Accounting for competitive performance, *Journal of Cost Management*, vol. 3, no.1, pp. 20–8
5 Nolan Norton Institute (1990), *Measuring Performance in the Organisation of the Future: A Research Study*, Nolan Norton: Boston MA

CHAPTER 9

Process improvement

The importance of focusing on the processes within a business is a consistent theme in this book. This is because of the impact they have in determining cost levels and the flexibility of the business to meet customer requirements at the right time. It is appropriate, therefore, to consider how specific techniques can assist in the improvement of process effectiveness. This chapter describes such techniques.

Business processes

It is fundamental to the management of any business that there is an understanding of what is taking place within the organisation and why. Only when there is this understanding of the business processes can improvements be made. These may take the form of improved quality and effectiveness or sustainable competitive advantage.

Quality improvements can be in both product and service delivery through an understanding of the complex linkages that exist in most business processes. Once these linkages and their impact on customers are understood, quality improvement programmes can be focused to gain maximum advantage.

Improved effectiveness can be measured in terms of either cost or time. Obtaining an understanding of the existing processes highlights areas of waste which can be minimised or eliminated. The time dimension of effectiveness is increasingly receiving the management attention it deserves, both in its own right and as a cause of cost. A reduction in process-time does not just lead to increased responsiveness and flexibility.

Competitive advantage can be created through an understanding of Michael Porter's[1] value chain and its application in managing the business processes for creating and sustaining a competitive position.

This concept is reinforced by the simple model of business design described in Chapter 2, which demonstrates that the formulation of strategy gives rise to objectives regarding product range, and targets customers and markets. Business processes are put in place to deliver this offering.

The reality of the central role played by business processes is therefore clear. Equally clear, however, is the fact that management reporting systems are generally very poorly focused to help manage these processes. Management is not equipped to understand how they behave. The traditional, financial-accounting-inspired cost reporting model is based on a vertical view of the business whereas business processes cut across departmental boundaries and tend to be **horizontal** in nature. Because processes usually cross many departmental responsibilities, they are often not properly managed and are poorly understood. The undertaking of a form of business process analysis may be the first time that senior management is able to compare, at the macro level, what is actually happening in the organisation with what should be happening, let alone consider whether the process can be improved or not.

Focusing on processes as a route to business improvement can be considered at three levels:

- The activity level: The efficiency with which individual activities which make up a process (such as placing purchase orders) are performed.
- The process level: The effectiveness of a whole process (such as the raw material procurement process).
- Between processes: The relationship between processes to optimise overall benefit (such that the raw material procurement process is synchronised, for example, with the production planning process).

Activity analysis is a good starting point for any exercise to effect process improvement for any of these levels. It provides a baseline for what is going on and how resources are being used. The technique for such analysis will be basically the same as for any use of activity costs described in this book; it can be performed in several ways, for example, by interviewing operational managers, by using questionnaires or by detailed observation of the activities. The use of direct interviews where possible is generally preferable as this enables the most sophisticated insight into what actually happens. Interviewers can identify:

- What can and does go wrong and the causes of problems; whether they are attributable to products, within processes, other departments, suppliers or customers.

- The informal links and cross-dependencies that are present within processes. These informal links are frequently not understood, let alone documented in any procedures manual. However, many business processes would not work if they were not present, as is illustrated by the potentially crippling effects of some 'work-to-rule' industrial action.
- What actually happens when problems arise in a process rather than what is supposed to happen. This is important in that it tends to build on the two issues mentioned above. The ability to cope with a problem illustrates the potential robustness of the business process to forces from both within and outside the organisation.

Such an insight is not possible with form-based analysis of processes.

Process improvement will now be considered at each of the three levels described above.

The activity level

When considering activities in the context of processes it is important to remember, as discussed in Chapter 3, that there is a difference between cost in the sense of **spending** to provide resources, and cost as the **consumption** of those resources by an activity. If an activity ceases to be performed the spending will often continue until management action is taken to avoid it by no longer providing the resources or by using the resources in a different way. In a similar manner spending may be in irregular lumps such as capacity on capital equipment or adding people to a department. When looking at process improvement it is primarily resource consumption that is being considered. Once the resource consumption implications of any change have been understood, the management decision-making process can switch to making changes in spending. So, whereas process changes may give rise to responsiveness improvements in the short term, changes to **spending** will vary with the nature of the resource and the practicality of being able to flex resource levels or switch them elsewhere.

In Chapter 4, the link was established between the activity and the product for product costing. While this helps to achieve an understanding of product costs, the risk of considering **only** this factor is that it could lead to dysfunctional decisions: for example, doubling batch sizes in an attempt to reduce set-up costs per unit of product.[2] This may be the reverse of longer term aims, such as shortening processing lead-times and reducing stocks. To effect process improvement, it is important then to consider the factors affecting the activity cost. This involves identifying the **cost input drivers**, the influences which determine how much resource is used to perform the activity. These may include such factors as product design, factory layout, operating procedures employed and labour/clerical productivity. Action plans then need to be developed for managing these factors in a way that will reduce costs.

Figure 9.1 is a duplicate of Figure 3.12 and provides a starting point for considering activity costs in the context of process improvement. Figure 9.2 shows this structure for the activity of batch testing in a food company. It shows a framework for understanding the factors that influence what resources are consumed by an activity within the business process. On the right-hand side of the diagram are the **activity drivers**, those factors which cause the activity to take place at all and which determine its frequency. The two questions that are asked are:

● What requires the activity to take place at all?

● What factors influence the frequency with which the activity takes place?

On the left-hand side of the diagram are the **input drivers**, those factors that influence the resource consumption when the activity takes place. The key question that is asked here is: 'Why is the activity carried out this way?'

In addition there is a covert question that must be asked for a full understanding of the activity: 'Why this activity at all? What does it add to the process?' (This last question is important in the identification of **negative activities**, discussed below.)

The production process for some types of pharmaceutical tablets provides another simple example of these two types of driver for an activity. The activity comprises the key step of granulating the active ingredients with bulking agents. A study at a tablet manufacturing facility highlighted the fact that the clean-down and set-up of the granulation machines was a bottleneck activity that limited the throughput of the facility significantly. In common with many pharmaceutical manufacturing processes, this clean-down and set-up is very important to ensure that ingredients from one tablet type do not contaminate other formulations that have been granulated in the same machines. The activity involves a total cleaning of all the components that come into contact with the ingredients, even including the filters on the extractor fans fitted to the dryers used in the process. In addition, regulatory requirements stipulate that the machines must be cleaned down between certain batches within a campaign to avoid the risk of cross-contamination between batches.

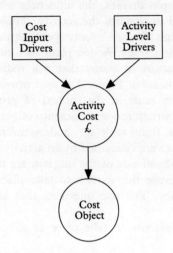

Figure 9.1 Factors that cause cost to occur.

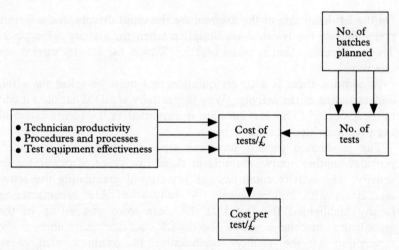

Figure 9.2 The Y diagram for batch testing in a food company.

The trigger for the cleaning activity is the decision to start a series of production runs for a particular tablet formulation. The factors that influence the frequency with which the activity takes place are twofold: the number of campaigns of tablet production that are planned and the number of batches processed within a campaign. These are the activity drivers.

The analysis of how the activity was carried out showed that at the start of the study the machines were fully dismantled by hand and all components washed and dried prior to reassembly under clean conditions. Thus the cost input drivers included the experience and motivation of the operatives and the defined procedure of complete stripdown. An attempt had been made to introduce new technology for the cleaning process, but it was not working correctly and capital expenditure to correct the problems had been deferred as it was not seen to be a critical project.

Why this activity at all? What does it add to the process? This activity is tightly controlled by various regulatory authorities such as the Department of Health in the United Kingdom and the US Food and Drugs Authority. Without proper cleaning of the equipment the manufacturer would be unable to manufacture or sell any tablets that require granulation as part of the manufacturing process.

The analysis showed that the activity was clearly unavoidable and that, while the bottleneck could be removed in the short term by increasing run lengths, there was no long term alternative to an investment in extra capacity or in the work required to automate fully the cleaning process. The key to process improvement was therefore in understanding the **cost drivers** and taking steps to increase throughput and reduce long run expenditure.

The process level

The **analysis of processes** to identify potential for improvement and redesign involves the use of activity mapping.[3] This is a two-staged exercise.

Step 1: Activity analysis to determine the activities that take place and the resources they consume.

Step 2: Linking the activities to processes as 'cost objects'.

Treating business processes as cost objects, when combined with activity analysis, results in an 'activity map' which aids the understanding of business processes and their impact on the cost base.

The first stage in activity mapping is to undertake a business process analysis using activity analysis as discussed above. To obtain full benefit from activity analysis for process improvement, it is essential to focus on three aspects:

● What causes the activity to take place as often as it does.

- Why the activity consumes as much resource as it does when the activity takes place.
- What the linkages are between activities (that is, the chain of activities that makes up the business process).

To understand the linkages between activities, it is necessary to ask the person who is responsible for the activity:

- Who and what triggers the activity to be performed?
- Upon whom are you dependent for information or product or service flow to enable you to perform the activity?
- What subsequent activities are triggered by the activity?
- Who is dependent on you to enable them to perform an activity?

These linkages, which may be between activities within the same or different departments, can then be used to display graphically the activities as a business process. The example shown in Figure 9.3 is a simplified version of part of a logistics process. This chart shows all activities that are part of the process of obtaining materials for manufacturing. The horizontal rows indicate the departments involved in the process and the boxes within the chart indicate activities. The first thing to notice is that even in this simplified version the chart looks very complicated. If the activity 'goods inwards' is further expanded to show what happens when an unexpected consignment is delivered to the store (Figure 9.4), it can be seen that the process of evaluation is very complex, involving stores, purchasing, production planning and quality assurance departments as well as the supplier. In this case, merely illustrating the complexity demonstrated the impact of operating with ill-defined responsibilities and caused management to address the issue.

The activity maps are annotated with the cost of each activity and, by addition, for the entire process in each department and in total (activity costs have not been shown in Figure 9.3 for reasons of space). As well as representing resource by cost, the chart can just as effectively reflect the consumption of time. This can be done by spacing the horizontal linkages to represent elapsed time using a consistent timescale for the whole chart. The technique is then used to identify potential for overall cycle-time reduction as part of achieving world-class standards and inventory reduction in the supply chain of a manufacturing business.

Different symbols or colours can be used in the chart to highlight various aspects of the business process such as the basic flow of activities

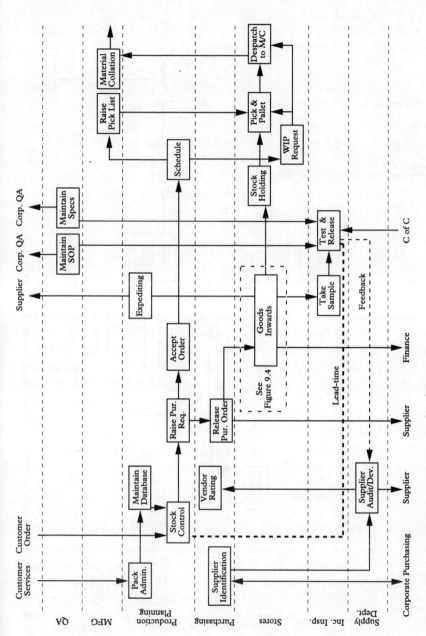

Figure 9.3 Material/component supply chain.

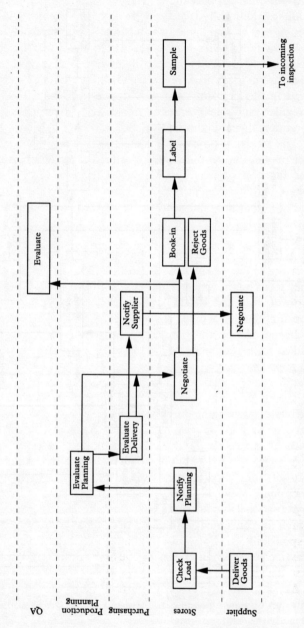

Figure 9.4 Goods-in: extra activities when consignment is not expected by system.

that are regularly associated with the process as opposed to those activities that support the process, for example, supplier evaluation and audits. Additionally, the activities that occur only when something goes wrong can be highlighted to illustrate the impact of non-conformance.

When the activity maps are drawn for the first time they should be validated with all key people involved and adjustments made. Corrections from the initial version will always be necessary because most departments perform some activities or are involved in linkages that are irregular, and the operational manager will have been unaware of or forgotten them in the first analysis.

The interview process will almost always throw up linkages that were not previously identified, and without which the present process would not function. It may also identify where there are 'dangling linkages' where one department believes that an activity is necessary for another but the other does not need or use it, such as an information report that takes a long time to prepare but is filed and never used.

Users of work-study process flowcharts will recognise these charts as an adaptation of the process flowchart technique. The differences are that the activity maps look at **activities** rather than at detailed tasks, and they focus on the linkages and **consumption of resources** rather than the type of task undertaken at each stage. Activity maps show resource consumption as activity costs.

In the example illustrated, the activity drivers for the core process are linked to the number of deliveries and the number of issues from stores to manufacturing. The question to ask is not: 'How can we reduce the number of transactions?' This is because the business is driving towards increased flexibility and reduced batch sizes with more frequent deliveries. The right question is revised to: 'How can we simplify the process so that we can handle the increased number of transactions without increasing the overall consumption of resources?' The activity map suggests various options that managers can explore to achieve the aim of simplicity and cost-effectiveness. The activity map gives a horizontal view of the business which is not distorted by the organisational boundaries. This compares to traditional cost reporting which is concerned with a vertical view based on departments and responsibilities. Forward-thinking organisations are now looking to reassign responsibilities to cover business processes, rather than to create new departments.

Activity maps provide a starting point for process improvement through **business process redesign**,[4] that is, the examination of the flow of activities and information that make up the key business processes in an organisation with a view to simplification, cost reduction or improvement in quality or flexibility.

Most business processes have never been designed, but have evolved over time to meet changing circumstances and to fix problems that have occurred historically. Many have evolved in an environment where control was more important than simplicity, flexibility and cycle-time. As a result there is often considerable scope for dramatic improvements in performance provided that managers and their advisers have the ability to ask the fundamental questions and answer them from many different perspectives.

Activity mapping, as described above, is a technique that raises such questions about the existing process from an activity perspective so that managers can take action to redesign the process. The term activity maps, rather than flowcharts, has been chosen to designate the use for which this technique is intended: for management to review the process with the aim of asking the question 'Why?' The maps show the manager where the process is now; the answers to the question will lead to a move in the right direction to improve the process through redesign.

The steps to redesign involve:

- Understanding what the process is supposed to deliver to the business
- Understanding the demands of the process so that account can be taken of resource requirements
- Understanding the present process in terms of activities and resource consumption
- Either altering the process in an evolutionary way by simplification and reduction in cross-departmental linkages that are no longer required, or
- Totally questioning the basis of the present process and altering the way people involved in the process think about their roles, so that a step change in performance can be achieved

The final stage is to perform a brainstorming exercise to consider alternative ways to redesign the process. Once an alternative design has been developed, the critical step is management commitment and action to implement the changes.

An example of identifying potential for improvement through activity mapping is provided by a major European airline, which undertook activity analysis of the work planning processes in its maintenance and engineering operations. During this study the following steps were identified:

- Engineering schedules were developed based on aircraft manufacturers' recommendations and airworthiness authorities' directives.

These schedules specify what work must be done on an aircraft and at which points in its operating life.

- Hangar schedules were developed to balance the optimum down-time of the aircraft with the availability of hangar slots and manpower. This planning process covered an extended time horizon with more detailed consideration given to the immediate twelve months.
- Planning schedules were developed to match the engineering schedules to the hangar schedules and to specify exactly what tasks should be undertaken in any aircraft visit.
- Operating schedules were developed that allocated the tasks to mechanics and specified the order and timing of each task.
- Work was undertaken against the schedules, which were adjusted on the hangar floor to cope with unforeseen circumstances.

During the study it became very apparent that the steps in this process were far from seamless. Each of the five steps described above was undertaken by separate departments with definite demarcation points. Each department undertook its activities in isolation once the previous department had passed on any relevant documentation or schedules, as if there were walls between the departments and data was being thrown over the walls. An example of this was that every department had its own rules of thumb on how long any combination of tasks should take. The result was that the lowest common denominator always prevailed and all parties ended up blaming the others when there were delays or aircraft were grounded with no available hangar space or manpower to work on them.

An examination of the activities in each department and the drivers for these activities also revealed that much work was being duplicated at each interface because vital information and assumptions were not being communicated properly. Source material was frequently passed to the next department who had to reassimilate and interpret it to discover if it was even relevant to them.

As a result of this study management was able to reassess the contribution of each department and changes were made both to the way information was communicated and to the organisational structure. The most significant of the changes was that engineering, who had access to manufacturers' recommended timings for each job, specified the time required for each task. This time is now used by all departments and only altered with experience when all parties agree that a change is necessary. The new approach also means that there is a feedback process to engineering based on task experience and learning. Other changes resulted in greater commitment to agreed schedules by mechanics and an increased understanding of the impact of delays.

The understanding of the key planning process led management to reassess the process and its impact on its customers. This resulted in improved on-time performance and communications, both within the organisation and with the end customer, the airline, which in turn was better able to plan its aircraft availability for flight schedules. In addition, the improved planning process has led to better use of existing resources and hence to long term sustainable cost reduction.

This case also illustrates a situation where failure to understand the fundamental process led to duplicated activities in different departments and a conflict with TQM objectives. The redesigned process removed the unnecessary duplications and created a greater sense of ownership across the business of the whole planning process. Changes in the way work was scheduled and controlled at the detail level also increased accountability and responsibility in the hangars.

No description of process improvement would be complete without reference to the concept of **value-added** and **non-value-added** activities. This is a concept developed largely by Japanese manufacturing companies such as Toyota. Value-added activities are those in the manufacturing process which add to customer satisfaction with the product. Non-value-added activities are those which do not, and are therefore waste, to be minimised or eliminated:

- Machine set-up is non-value-added (as the machine is not making anything while being set up). Management should therefore seek to minimise set-up cost, and set targets each year to do so by, for example, better production planning to achieve partial set-up, product design to minimise the number and complexity of tools needed and investment in more flexible machines.
- Logistics in the factory is another non-value-added activity (moving a product does not make it more valuable). Therefore the factory will be laid out to minimise the need for movement.
- Inspection is non-value-added. Therefore the product will be designed, the operator trained and the production process set up to eliminate the need for inspectors.
- Stockholding is non-value-added. Therefore a JIT philosophy will prevail.

It is this constant focus on eliminating non-value-added activity which has helped make Japanese manufacturers so successful. The traditional Western approach has been to optimise, rather than minimise. Thus batch set-up cost is optimised against stockholding cost to achieve an economic batch size. This approach accepts the level of waste (machine set-up and stockholding cost) instead of minimising it.

Between processes

From the foregoing sections it will be apparent that business processes are often complex, haphazard and, of prime importance, dependent on each other. Also, processes will inevitably include activities that are non-value-added. The concept of **value-added** and **non-value-added** activities has become well known, and has largely originated from Japan. The distinction between the two is simply one of whether the activity directly adds to meeting the customer's expectation of what the product will do. Thus, machining is value-added, whereas setting up a machine is not. Many businesses have made large cost savings and effected huge manufacturing efficiencies through a rigorous programme to reduce and eliminate non-value-added activities. Indeed, just-in-time is principally concerned with precisely this. Activity analysis and activity mapping of processes can provide very real support to such programmes. In some cases, non-value-added activities are the result of poor plant layout, poorly designed processes and bad practice. These tend to be relatively easy to eradicate. The more difficult non-value-added activities are those which appear to be essential if the business is to continue functioning. Such activities are frequently added to business processes in a reactive way in response to problems. This results in **symptoms**, rather than the **underlying causes**, being addressed.

In these circumstances they can be called **negative activities**.[5] Examples of this type of negative activity are expediting and work rescheduling, as shown in Figure 9.5. There are many examples of businesses where whole departments have grown up to undertake these tasks, while the causes of the need for them are never even examined: the need for the activity is assumed to be a fact of life. Thus, negative activities are not only non-value-added in their own right, but they cause

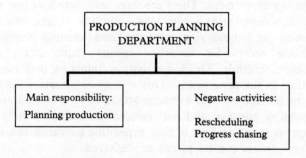

Figure 9.5 Negative activities are a response to problems.

many other non-value-added activities to occur. It is not possible, however, merely to stop expediting; it is a symptom of something being wrong and the underlying cause of the problem has to be put right. Furthermore, negative activities nearly always occur when something is wrong in another process in the business. They are an indicator of problems **between processes** and show that the value of the business is suboptimal.

The example below concerns a hypothetical company, Chaos Ltd, and illustrates how negative activities not only waste effort where they occur but also have an impact throughout the entire value chain.

Chaos Ltd is a medium-sized engineering firm that specialises in very high precision machining and subassembly work for the aerospace and automotive industries. Although the workforce is very busy, Chaos Ltd is losing money and has cashflow difficulties. In addition, relationships with suppliers and customers are suffering due to constant changes in production schedules.

In an effort to improve performance, an activity analysis exercise is undertaken with the following results:

- Customer services department: Analysis of this department shows that there are two major activities that take place. The first is entering new orders and confirming acceptance to customers with a committed delivery date. This activity takes about a quarter of the department's effort. The second activity, which takes about three-quarters of the department's effort, is expediting customer orders that are behind the original committed delivery date or which the customer needs urgently. A culture has developed in customer services that rewards the ability to meet customer requirements in all cases. While this is a desirable goal, the result has been that fire-fighting has become normal and people in this department take pride in making the shipment against all the odds.
- Purchasing department: There are three main activities that take place within this department – negotiating purchase orders with suppliers; evaluating and qualifying potential and existing suppliers; and expediting orders for material urgently required for the daily production schedule. This last activity accounts for over two-thirds of the effort in the department. This activity has increased dramatically over the last few months as buffer stocks have been used up (to help the cashflow position) and not replaced. In addition, the purchasing manager is spending a lot of time expediting payments to suppliers so that new orders can be placed or delivered.
- Scheduling department: This department is involved in constantly replanning the production schedule to meet customer requirements.

The constant pressure from customer services department and capacity constraints mean that there is little real planning at all, as orders are scheduled in the knowledge that the sequence of work will change several times prior to delivery.

- Tooling department: This department is responsible for setting up machine tools for production and providing new tools as required. However, analysis suggests that a high proportion of set-ups are wasted for the following reasons:

  - Changes to the production schedule mean that the set-up is no longer required and machines need to be reset for different production requirements.
  - An expedited works order requires that machines are reset in the middle of another order and then reset again for that order once the expedited order is completed.
  - Poor scheduling means that orders are not processed in an order that would minimise the required set-up effort while meeting output requirements.

- Production department: This department is involved in the production of works orders, but a significant amount of time is spent in moving materials to and from the machine shops as the production schedule changes, and waiting for machine tools to be set up for the next production order.

Customers have been giving complex work to Chaos knowing that they have unique skills that provide the required product quality and accuracy. In addition, Chaos have historically been able to respond to very short lead-times required for prototype or design changes. However, customers have started to place simpler, long run orders with other suppliers who have better delivery performance. Alternative suppliers of high accuracy machining are being sought but would appear to be significantly more expensive.

The above suggests that the scheduling process is the cause of a lot of negative activities throughout Chaos: better planning and scheduling would appear to be required. This would lead to less fire-fighting by customer services and purchasing, and fewer wasted set-ups with their consequent reduction in capacity. It is only by getting the scheduling process right that the other processes can be effective. The sales order process, for example, may be excellent, but the relationship **between processes** is causing it to be suboptimal.

It is important to consider why this situation has arisen before redesigning the scheduling process. Failure to do so will mean that any steps taken for process improvement will inevitably fail. Chaos has a business problem in that they do not recognise where they are adding value for their customers. The culture of the customer services department will need to change so that they become part of the planning process by working with customers to anticipate changes in requirements. If this does not happen the negative activities here will continue to drive wasted effort in other areas which will continue the cost escalation and further disrupt production to the point that customers switch to more expensive alternative suppliers.

There would appear to be a number of common causes of negative activities. The most common are:

- A manufacturing lead-time which is incompatible with customers' requirements
- An organisational structure that is no longer appropriate for the business environment
- Poor logistics flow
- A badly designed bill of materials, especially in an MRP or MRPII environment
- Historical quality problems that have not been properly addressed
- Organisational cultures that thrive on fire-fighting with very little long term planning
- Management culture and style

The last item above is very important. Douglas McGregor's[6] well-known research describes two management cultures termed Theory X and Theory Y. Theory X assumes that all employees are basically idle and dishonest and require close supervision and control. On the other hand Theory Y assumes that employees are basically honest and will work to achieve common goals with sufficient support and empowerment. C.J. McNair[7] has argued that traditional cost management has tended to assume Theory X while more recent approaches such as activity-based management have tended to assume Theory Y.

Under a Theory X management culture activities may be added as controls and audits. While these activities may consume resources they may not be regarded as negative by management in that they are part of the normal control system. However, in a Theory Y culture these activities have a negative impact on the value-adding processes and they can be regarded as negative activities. An example of this would be multiple levels of authorisation for routine transactions. The results of this could be:

- The business process is slower than needed due to the need to wait for signatures

- Employees have reduced self-esteem and do not check for errors as they know these will be corrected later
- Poor control as the authorisations become routine and fail in their intended audit role
- A climate that suppresses innovation and change that could benefit the organisation if properly harnessed

The important factor to consider when negative activities are encountered is the underlying cause of them: they are symptomatic of a business problem that has not been properly addressed.

References

1 M.E. Porter (1985), *Competitive Advantage: Creating and Sustaining Superior Performance*, Free Press: New York
2 H.T. Johnson, Thomas P. Vance and R. Steven Player (1990), Pitfalls in using ABC cost-driver information to manage operating costs, *Corporate Controller*, vol. 3, no. 2
3 M. Morrow and M. Hazell (1992), Activity mapping for business process redesign, *Management Accounting Magazine* (CIMA), vol. 70, no. 2, pp. 36–8
4 M. Hammer (1990), Re-engineering work: don't automate, obliterate, *Harvard Business Review*, Reprint 90406, vol. 68, no. 4, pp. 104–12
5 The concept of negative activities as described was jointly developed by KPMG Management Consulting and Waldron Galloway
6 D. McGregor (1960), *The Human Side of Enterprise*, McGraw-Hill: Maidenhead
7 C.J. McNair (1990), Responsibility Redefined: Activity Accounting and the Learning Organisation, Rhode Island University, CAMI contracted report R88CM209, February

CHAPTER 10

Systems and implementation issues

The previous chapters of this book laid out an agenda for performance measurement and cost management to support the implementation of competitive strategy, the effectiveness of manufacturing operations and processes, and an understanding of the contribution to profitability of products, customers and marketplaces in which companies compete. An essential ingredient in delivering this agenda is the design, development and implementation of cost management and performance measurement systems. Given the diverse nature of the requirements a standard formula for such systems cannot be expected and this chapter describes the issues that arise for system design and implementation.

The term cost management system is used in this chapter to mean a mechanism for delivering information regarding all aspects of the cost base of an organisation and, for convenience, will be used in addition to denote performance measurement systems.

The challenges in delivering cost management systems can be summarised as being concerned with the following issues:

- Determining the scope: What is the scope of the system? Should the system be broad in scope or focused on a few key issues? Should the high level competitive and strategic issues be addressed or the operational control and performance management issues? Should there be a single system that aims to deliver the whole cost management agenda?
- Choosing between multiple and sometimes conflicting priorities: Difficulties are faced in deciding where attention should be focused. Should the system satisfy the planning and strategy director, the marketing director, the operations director or the finance director? The priorities of the information seekers in the organisation can impact on the design of the system.
- Determining timing and timescales: Having decided the priorities, the

timing with which these requirements will be satisfied can be determined. Should a core system be built that may last for five or ten years? This may involve a full mainframe implementation and take two years to complete. Instead, should a project be pursued that will give some answers in two to three months? Such a project may involve a PC-based solution.

- Addressing changing business needs: Business information needs change with the external forces affecting the nature of competition and the items on the management agenda. How flexible a system is required if it is to be driven by parameters that change to meeting changing business needs? Competitive responses to changes in competitor rivalry, barriers to entry, and the relative power of buyers and suppliers will involve changes in the products offered, distribution channels used, customers served, markets covered and technology used.

- Coping with the limitation of the cost of systems: What level of expenditure on the system is justified? If the system is intended to address a wide range of issues and if the requirement is to build a system that is long term, complex and flexible, the limitations imposed by cost must be considered even more carefully than usual. The cost of implementation should be weighed against the benefits. Large and broadly-based systems will have significant implications for the hardware, software, degree of integration between systems, processing capacity and power, and the configuration of the system (PCs, terminals, printers, etc.). The cost of such implementations can be prohibitive.

- Creating different solutions for different business environments: What should the response time be for the system? Is the system intended to provide real-time performance information or will information updated weekly suffice? The answer lies in the decisions that are being made and is therefore likely to be a function of the nature of the business environment. Markets where real-time decisions are required (e.g. retailing) will require real-time systems. For stable and largely predictable market environments, traditional batch processing systems perhaps largely driven by the monthly, quarterly and annual accounting cycle may suffice.

- Ensuring appropriate sponsorship and ownership: Should the sponsors be the accountants, the marketers, the planners or the manufacturing operators? Who actually owns the system? Without appropriate sponsorship and ownership the system will fail.

These and other systems design and implementation issues will be addressed in this chapter.

Four-stage systems migration path

Robert Kaplan[1] has identified a four-stage migration path for the development of cost management systems. This provides a good framework for starting considering system issues. The steps in the migration path are as follows:

- Phase 1: traditional systems. These are typified as having poor data quality in large volumes and provided too late to enable corrective action to be taken. They are largely driven by financial reporting requirements (such as stock valuation). In such systems product costs include extensive volume-based arbitrary allocations. Operational control information consists of extensive financial variances.
- Phase 2: advanced traditional systems. These are typically an improvement over the Phase 1 systems in that the data quality is much improved, is precise, timely and focused. However, they too tend to be based on satisfying financial reporting requirements. Again, product costs include extensive volume-based arbitrary allocations. Operational control information is rationalised and includes reporting of financial variances on an exception basis.
- Phase 3: parallel systems. Here it is recognised that new information systems are needed and these are developed to run alongside existing systems. Therefore they can be developed and prototyped without worrying about being unable to meet existing reporting requirements. They tend to be PC-based and configured with shared databases or linked stand-alone systems with reporting frequency determined by user requirements. The Phase 2 system is used for the satisfaction of regular financial reporting, and the parallel systems are used for delivering whatever new applications are required. These might be, for example, the development of activity-based product costs, customer profitability analysis, activity-based budgets or a balanced scorecard of performance measures.
- Phase 4: integration. In this phase the parallel systems development in Phase 3 is integrated into the companies' main systems to become a regular part of management reporting. Typically, Phase 4 will involve configuring integrated databases and systems, and some elements of the old systems will be dropped. The provision of financial reporting requirements and cost management information is then combined into one set of systems.

Not all businesses follow this four-phase migration. Many develop Phase 3 parallel applications and find this a perfectly acceptable solution for providing the additional information they require. Others feel that parallel systems cause confusion and give conflicting messages and will move straight to changing their main company systems (although, if this approach is chosen, prototyping is still advisable).

An example of the issues surrounding the use of parallel systems can be found in one of Hewlett Packard's divisions. It recognised that the nature of its business had dramatically changed since the implementation of its costing system. Direct labour represented only about 5% of its total cost, but its costing system continued to allocate overheads to products on the basis of direct labour content.

This resulted in marketing and production management losing faith in the information produced by the finance department. The research and development department grew increasingly frustrated with designing out labour cost without any resulting reduction in total overall costs, as the overhead burden rates merely increased to offset the labour reductions. The production department felt that the accounting system averaged the costs of producing complex and low volume products across all products, and therefore caused the marketing department to price these products poorly and to misinterpret product profitability.

Given the cross-functional interest in the results of the costing system and the way in which these affected the behaviour of the functions it was felt that a multidisciplinary team was required. The terms of reference of the team were to examine the nature of the business at an activity level, to determine the cost drivers of the activities and to identify the consumption of resources by activity. A PC-based activity-based product costing model was then built to utilise this information.

The research and development and production departments identified with the new approach and found the new information very useful. However, since the financial reporting figures and product profitability information were still being produced from the old system, monitoring of the business's performance from outside the division continued to be against the old figures. The presence of two sets of conflicting figures regarding the same subject caused confusion and it was felt that the use of the old figures resulted in incorrect decision-making. Because of this, the division decided to scrap the parallel systems and adopt an integrated system using the activity-based approach. They now find that the messages from their information systems are consistent across functions and the cost of products reflects the resources expended.

Hewlett Packard migrated from a parallel PC system to an integrated mainframe system. Some fundamental lessons about their information requirements, the appropriateness of the design of the system's cost drivers, and the decisions that they expected managers to take were learnt on the PC system before the migration. They continued to make incremental changes to their system after live running to simplify the design and reflect changes in the business.

It should be recognised that the practical difference in the design approach between Phase 3 systems and Phase 4 systems is largely to do with the rigour and formalisation of the analysis. Phase 4 systems tend to be more capital-expensive and generally involve a more structured approach to systems design and implementation. In contrast Phase 3 systems range between simple decision support tools on PCs to stand-alone models linked into the core systems. This does not mean that Phase 3 systems do not provide critical information for fundamental business decisions. The approach applicable to Phase 3 systems is broadly the same as Phase 4; the difference is in the operating environment of the system and the disciplines surrounding its use.

Predesign considerations

Prior to designing and implementing cost management systems, it is important to consider the issues that will affect the success of the project. Robin Cooper identified six major decisions that need to be made before an ABC system can be implemented.[2] These are as follows and are valid for any cost management or performance measurement system:

- Should the system be integrated with the existing system or should it be a stand-alone system?
- Should a formal design be approved before implementation?
- Who should take 'ownership' of the final system?
- How precise should the system be?
- Should the system report historical or future costs?
- Should the initial design be complex or simple?

The issues from each of these questions are now considered in turn.

The need to build the cost management system into the existing systems and the degree of integration required

This affects the cost of the implementation, the degree of future flexibility and the speed with which the system can be introduced and then tailored in future. The issues to consider include assessing the likelihood that the information requirements will change materially in the future. This is determined largely by the following:

- The extent to which the requirements are well established.
- The dynamism of the business environment. If the environment is

largely predictable and static then there is less need for the flexibility of a stand-alone system.
- The diversity of the users relying on the systems. Where fewer people are reliant on the system there may be less chance of the requirements changing.

In addition, where a stand-alone system is dependent for most of its data from a multitude of existing systems, the importance of the timing and frequency for updating the data can result in greater effectiveness if the system is integrated with the existing systems and handled by a data processing department.

The degree of formalisation required

Traditional structured approaches to the implementation of mini-computer and mainframe systems typically involve the submission of formal design and implementation papers to users. The many published case studies in the implementation of PC-based cost management systems show that such formal steps are rarely necessary given the low cost of such PC systems, the speed with which such systems can be introduced and the experimentation needed in the design stage, typically through the use of prototypes. The decision regarding the degree of formalisation should be a function of the following:

- The size of the audience for the system. Unless large numbers are involved, the use of brief presentations, and 'walking' through the system design and output based on a prototype, is usually better than a formal document.
- The cost management application to be undertaken. One-off decision support tools and systems which are not a part of routine reporting rarely require formal design and implementation papers (although this is not to say that they do not require auditing to check integrity).
- The reliability and experience of the project manager. If reliance can be placed on the project manager to involve the relevant parties and consider their views then formal design and implementation papers would not be required on most Phase 3 systems.
- The speed with which results are required. If the cost management system is required as a matter of urgency, for example, to support a make or buy decision, then the time to exercise the strictness of such formal steps may not be available.
- The degree to which it is recognised that system development will be an iterative process whereby users assess usefulness and design as the project progresses.

Sponsorship and ownership

Without appropriate senior management commitment to the project, management will not use the information for decision-making. Without ensuring 'buy-in' from the users by taking a multi-interest group approach to creating the design and implementation team, the system may be ill-conceived and lack credibility. A cost management system should not be an 'accounting system created by accountants for accountants'.

The precision of the system

The degree of precision in the information provided depends on the purpose of the cost management system. In any event, it is better to be approximately right than precisely wrong.

The type of cost reported

The relevance of historic costs in cost management systems has often been questioned. However, as Robert Kaplan has pointed out[3] a cost management system can be used to process whatever data the user desires. That is, a good cost management system provides a model of cost behaviour for processing inputs in a certain manner and delivering output in a predetermined form. Such a system can be fed with historic costs, average costs, forecast or planned costs, opportunity costs or whatever costs the user requires.

The degree of system design complexity

The complexity is determined by the structure of the business, the application for which the system is designed, and finally the need to reflect the business processes in sufficient detail that it is credible as a system. The use of prototypes can help to establish the degree of complexity required.

Systems design and implementation approach

The typical stages in cost management systems design and implementation are those used in generic approaches and can be expected in all system design and implementation projects, whether the subject is cost management, accounting systems or operational systems. Some of these steps are of greater importance in certain types of applications. In designing information systems, such as cost management systems, the critical emphasis should be on the definition of **business issues** and the resulting **information and decision requirements**. This point cannot be overemphasised; the value of a cost measurement system is only in its ability to help managers make decisions relevant to the issues they face. If nothing changes as a result of information from the system, it has no value as a management tool.

A generic approach to the design and implementation of cost management systems typically involves the following steps:

- Identifying the nature of the business requirement
- Specifying information requirements
- Designing the system
- Identifying, evaluating and selecting the systems solution including prototyping
- Implementing the system
- Roll-out and use

Some of the above steps would be inappropriate in some circumstances, for example, for a company seeking a cost management decision support tool for a one-off decision.

Identifying the nature of the business requirement

Without a clear idea of what the cost management system is designed to deliver it is not possible to create an effective solution. The implementation of a concept or approach (for example, activity-based product costing, activity-based budgeting, throughput accounting) rather than a solution to a business problem (poor profitability analysis, large increases in overheads year on year, poor scheduling) results in a system that very quickly becomes irrelevant. Therefore the starting point for the exercise is the definition of the nature of the business problem or problems that the cost management system is aiming to address. Symptoms that existing systems are not meeting all the requirements include:

- Low profitability relative to competitors and loss of profitable market share: Where a company is failing to price its products competitively, despite having exercised good overhead cost management, it is possible that the existing costing system is cross-subsidising complex products with a systematic bias against simple products. Arbitrary cost allocations result in simple products having a share of overheads that is not commensurate with their consumption. If this occurs in an industry where pricing decisions are a function of cost, the company will steadily lose market share in its simple products and gain unprofitable market share in its complex products.

- Losing competitive tenders in areas believed to be strengths: Where managers find it difficult to explain the reasons for winning and losing competitive bids because of price, it is likely that the costing system is not revealing the true cost of the work involved.
- Managers develop their own costing systems: If line managers lose faith in the costing system and develop their own decision support costing systems, it is likely that the relevance of the costing system needs to be examined.

Robin Cooper summarised the events[4] which may mean the approach to cost management systems needs to be reviewed. These include the following:

- An increased use of automation.
- The demands placed on support functions change dramatically.
- The product-market strategy is changed.
- The manufacturing process is changed or simplified.
- The intensity of rivalry increases, accentuating the importance of better intelligence regarding the internal and external position.
- Deregulation allows competitive pricing.
- Technological improvements result in changes to the business process.
- Changes in business strategy, for example, from cost minimisation to differentiation.

To ensure that options are not closed too early on in defining the aims and objectives of the cost management system, it is necessary to begin by taking an exploratory requirements analysis approach – that is, identifying the problem by firstly assessing whether any of the above symptoms are evident and, secondly, undertaking an assessment of the relative competitive position of the business. Such an assessment enables management to understand the business's competitive strengths and weaknesses and the areas that are, or should be, the likely focus of their attention.

In seeking to implement a cost management system, it is important not to be tempted to stray into the arena of strategy analysis and formulation. The aim of the analysis described above is to ensure:

- The early recognition of fundamental mismatches between the strategy and business plan (the long term direction of the business) and the activities and consumption of resources in delivering that strategy.

- That options are not closed before the information requirements have been identified.
- That the level of detail likely to be required is ascertained. For example, if the business issues are strategic rather than operational, strategic information may be more summarised and approximate than operational information.
- That the mix of internal and external information required is ascertained. For example, where a company has a 'follow the leader' strategy, it may need to match the market leader on cost as well as product attributes. In such cases there is a need to include an information requirement for external cost benchmarking information on the product range of the leader.

Again, it is important not to undertake detailed analysis to find the problem if it can be articulated and easily verified at the outset.

Specifying information requirements

Having defined the nature of the business issue, the information required can be determined. Some information requirements will emerge automatically from the high level analysis of the issue. In a full analysis completeness would be ensured by undertaking the following:

- Identifying the dimensions of the business: The dimensions of the business include products, customers, distribution channels, markets, business units and geographical scope. These are the primary fields in which success can be measured and therefore along which information may be required.
- Relating the dimensions of the business to the company's cost structure: The cost structure would be expressed in terms of the hierarchy of costs as described in earlier chapters.
- Evaluating the success of the strategy in terms of the profitability of products, customers, distribution channels and markets: Initially, this information is likely to be decision-provoking as it reveals areas of low profitability. As management becomes accustomed to the information it will become decision-supporting. The production of this information will assist in challenging the existing information provided to management and assessing their requirements for profitability analysis.
- Defining the decisions that management expects to take: For each dimension of the business, the timing of such decisions and the extent to which certain types of information would influence or provoke those decisions. This information spans strategic and operational information.

The output from this stage should be a definition of the information requirements based on the business issues in terms of audience, form, content, level of accuracy, timing and frequency.

Designing the system

In this context the term system is used to encapsulate the procedures and suite of software and hardware that deliver the information requirement. The steps involved in designing the system are given below.

1. Segregating the system into application modules: Potentially, each distinct information requirement could have its own application module. For example, the manufacturing cost management information requirements may be handled through the development of the existing MRPII system and the product marketing requirements may be satisfied through the development of a database that feeds off existing operational and financial systems to analyse profitability by product within each customer order.
2. Determining the relationship between the modules: Having segregated the requirements into applications, an information map is required to ensure the following:

   • A clear specification of the flow of information
   • The integrity of the information
   • Reconciliation to the source data

3. Determining the data sources for each module: The information map should be enhanced to include the data sources of all the information needed to satisfy requirements. This will enable gaps to be identified.
4. Determining the data capture and feed methods including the degree of integration required between feeder systems and the cost management system: At this stage consideration needs to be given as to how information is to be collected. Hewlett Packard have described how their implementation of an activity-based cost management system at one of their plants was achieved without the collection of any new data, relying totally on their current information sources and systems to provide information. This may not be possible in all businesses. However, the principle remains valid. The degree of integration should be decided based upon considerations of efficiency and the need to avoid re-inputting.
5. Determining the outputs required from each module to satisfy the information requirements: At this stage the form and content of management reports should be defined.

The approach taken by a division of British Aerospace to address the design and development of a cost management system demonstrates how evolutionary phases can be used to combine an initial exploratory stage with a formal implementation stage. In the exploratory stage, British Aerospace commissioned a pilot study to establish the feasibility and benefits of an activity-based costing system. This involved determining information requirements and building a prototype PC system to demonstrate the appropriateness of the approach.

The key information requirements that the prototype system was designed to address included:

- Measuring contract costs to support pricing and profitability decisions
- Supporting 'make or buy' decisions, which are a recurrent feature of the company's operations
- Providing performance measurement data for both direct and support departments

By taking a small area of the business and building a prototype using a spreadsheet, it was possible to show how the relevant information could be structured and the activity-based principles applied to the business. At this stage a presentation was made to the board and approval given to move to the next stage of constructing a more substantial PC model. This operated in the following manner:

- As with the existing system, contract costs consisted of direct labour, direct materials and overheads.
- As with the existing system, direct labour and direct material were booked direct to the contract.
- Unlike the existing system, overheads were attributed to contracts on bases which recognised the true demand they placed on the company. This was achieved by holding activities, cost drivers, volumes of cost drivers and consumption of activities in the system.
- Unlike the existing system, a distinction was drawn between the levels of cost in the business. The system analysed costs into a hierarchy comprising contract attributable costs, facility-sustaining costs, site-sustaining costs and company-sustaining costs. It was demonstrated how this information could be used for contract costing, pricing and profitability analysis, to support make or buy decisions and performance measurement, by understanding the reality of cost behaviour.

The PC model covered a bigger part of the business and was able to handle quite large volumes of data. Through the use of the model, many valuable lessons were learnt about data sources, the level of detail required and how activities and cost drivers should be constructed and reported. At the end of this stage, again board approval was sought to continue with full implementation.

The company realised the importance of a multidirectorate working party to take the project forward and pursued the next stages as follows:

- Arranged a roll-out programme to secure the commitment of all managers.
- Set up a multidirectorate working party to take the initiative forward.
- Developed a full-blown activity-based reporting system. This was executed in three phases as follows:

  - Building a contract costing module concerned with contract attributable costs
  - Incorporating the three additional levels of sustaining costs
  - Integrating the system with the mainframe systems

The new information forms an important part of the division's thrust to obtain greater awareness and control of costs at the operating level, to match resource levels to activity levels and to engender an attitude of continuous improvement.

Systems solutions

The selection of software solutions will vary according to the information requirement being considered. Satisfying the total consideration may involve the provision of a mix of systems solutions from those described below. The four options for implementing a cost management system are as follows:

- As a one-off exercise: This will typically be appropriate if the aim is to support a one-off decision to make a sudden impact on the organisation.
- Ad hoc: A system run on an ad hoc basis, either in parallel or stand-alone, is often the appropriate solution when strategic decisions are to be made or the information is to be used as a benchmark to adjust performance.
- In parallel: In such a situation the cost management system would become a regular part of the company's procedures but does not take the place of the mainstream costing system. The cost management system can be used for decision-making whereas the mainstream system is used primarily for financial accounting purposes.
- Replacement: In such a case the new cost management principles replace the existing accounting and management reporting principles.

The types of software to consider include the following:

- Accounting packages: Standard accounting general ledger packages can be adapted to deliver the core cost management information by using the account code to collect cost information in cost pools, using the cost allocation module to assign costs to activities based on cost drivers and grouping activity costs to report, for example, product, customer, channel and market levels of cost.
- Packaged activity-based cost management systems: Packages on the market today offer analysis in the form of product costing, customer profitability, market segment profitability, activity costing, business process reporting, cost of non-value-added activities and financial and non-financial performance indicators in the form of cost driver analysis. Such systems rely on feeds from existing systems or the input of data.
- Creating bespoke cost management systems using multidimensional databases, spreadsheets and executive information systems: Simpler and more focused applications are generally PC-based and address-specific decision support applications. In such cases the appropriate tools tend to be spreadsheets or databases. Databases have the advantage of providing more durable solutions. However, spreadsheets tend to provide solutions faster and at lower cost. They are often appropriate for one-off decisions.

Information for strategic analysis and decision support tends to be more summarised and less frequent and either takes its feeds from more detailed operational systems, such as the manufacturing systems and the accounting systems, or from a stand-alone business model. In both cases the strategic cost management information system is likely to involve a modelling of the dimensions of the business to provide a wider view of the business and allow scenario analysis based on the variation of key business variables, such as manufacturing throughput, change in customer demand, change in prices, change in bought-in costs, reduction in manpower, discontinuation of product lines, customer or market segments. Again, proprietary PC-based modelling tools can be very effective vehicles for such systems.

Implementing the system

Research into the design and implementation of systems shows that common reasons why implementations fail are as follows:

- Inappropriate sponsorship: The cost management system should address fundamental issues concerning the business. As such it requires senior management, preferably board level, sponsorship if it is to be given sufficient importance within the organisation.

- Lack of ownership by target users: To ensure that target users 'buy in' to the project, it is important that they are involved sufficiently in the specification, design and implementation of the cost management system. As described earlier in this chapter, it is suggested that the key users should be part of the project team responsible for the system.
- Poor implementation support: This is especially true in the installation of packaged software. The apparent simplicity of installing a package masks the fact that its implementation has to be managed and that the main measure of success will be how well the system fits into the business and meets the primary information requirements.
- Poor specification of requirements. The steps outlined in this chapter should assist in overcoming problems in this area and in particular the question of user involvement and identification of business issues.
- Poor integration of systems: This can also be overcome through comprehensive mapping and analysis of feeder systems, as outlined above.
- Organisational issues: A number of organisational issues impact on the outcome of a project, including the lack of cohesion between different functions within a company, a corporate culture that does not emphasise delivery of projects to required specifications and conflicting priorities placed on project team members to the detriment of the project.

Having addressed the above potential pitfalls, the implementation plan for the system should include the following:

- Clarifying with the wider user community the business issues being addressed and also the management concepts that the system is based upon, such as activity-based approaches or the idea of a balanced scorecard for performance measurement.
- Involving users in prototyping and testing, including reasonableness tests.
- Discussion and agreement of what users are expected to do with the outputs from the cost management system. This is one of the most critical aspects of implementation. The primary aim of the project is not to create an elegant and technically robust solution; it is to provide solutions that will change behaviour, allow management to make decisions, and ultimately improve the performance of the business.
- Demonstration of benefits of implementation. A post-implementation assessment should be made to assess the impact the system has made

on the organisation's performance and to assess whether the original aims and objectives have been achieved.

Activity-based approaches

The general design and implementation process described so far provides a generic framework for handling specific applications, either as a project addressing a single application or multiple applications. Given the importance of activity-based approaches, the issues arising specifically from their use will now be discussed.

All activity-based systems are based on the following key concepts:

- The definition of activities: The system should have the facility to hold activity definitions and descriptions.
- The collection of activity costs: These costs may be taken directly from the existing general ledger classification or fed first into a module within the system to allow reanalysis and regrouping.
- The definition of activity levels (how often the activity takes place) and the source of such data.
- The definition of activity centres: This may be used to aggregate activities having a common theme to facilitate subsequent analysis, for example, all activities in the material supply chain or activities associated with the finance function.
- The definition of the cost levels within the business: For example, the units, batches, processes, sites, products, customers, distribution channels, market segments and others. Each activity has to fit within one of these levels.
- The consumption of activities by cost objects, and the source of this data: For example, if issuing a works order is defined as an activity, for activity-based product costing the system has to know how many works orders each product requires. Another example would be attributing a number of sales orders to a customer.
- The ability to 'flag' activities: Giving activities a flag to denote an attribute such as value-added or non-value-added, discretionary or essential, etc., can be very useful in subsequent analysis.
- Retaining the integrity of 'cost build-up' within activities: As described in Chapter 3, it is important to be able to understand the elements of cost within an activity in the final analysis, because this improves the understanding of how spending will change with activity levels.

It is important to note that activity-based systems typically hold much data and can produce very useful analysis if they are well structured.

An important issue in the design of many activity-based systems is the source of the base cost data. As outlined above, the cost pools for activity costs can be formed straight from general ledger line items, or via existing cost reports. Figure 10.1 shows these two approaches where the cost object is products. A similar point is illustrated in the requirement for department activity costs, shown in Figure 10.2. In this example,

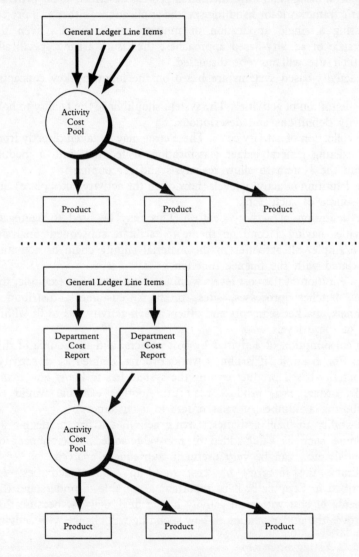

Figure 10.1 Forming an activity cost pool from general ledger line items or existing cost reports.

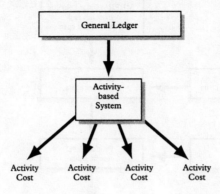

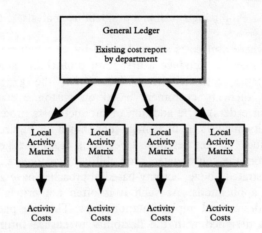

Figure 10.2 Deriving departmental activity costs.

activity costs can either be calculated centrally and delivered locally or, alternatively, existing departmental cost reports are delivered locally and then put through local 'activity matrices' (perhaps run on spreadsheets) to produce activity costs.

The feed of operational data into activity-based systems also has to be considered. Figure 10.3 shows how a customer profitability analysis (as discussed in Chapter 5) could be produced. Product cost comprising direct labour and direct materials are down-loaded from an existing standard costing or MRPII system into an activity-based model. Here, indirect product costs are allocated to activities and then to products. This cost per product is then fed into the product level profitability

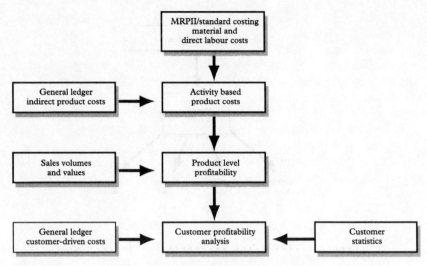

Figure 10.3 Producing a customer profitability analysis.

module where unit costs are multiplied by sales volumes and compared to sales values, to produce a first level profitability analysis. The final module takes customer-driven costs from the general ledger and attributes them to customers based on customer statistics (such as number of orders). The addition of product costs produces a customer profitability analysis. A final stage (not shown on Figure 10.3) might be to introduce market segment level costs from the general ledger to deduct from the consolidated profitability of customers in that segment.

As illustrated above, activity-based approaches have a broad range of potential applications. As such it is often not critical to go through rigorous design and implementation steps. This is especially true if the system is designed with the flexibility to ensure future access to the information required. The use of certain types of software is likely to close the options at an early stage. For example, the use of spreadsheets is likely to limit the number of applications that the system can support, while the use of a multidimensional database or ABC package will allow migration to other applications if they are implemented with the wider applications in mind.

Conclusions

This chapter has outlined the factors that must be managed, and the types of approach which can be adopted, in order to design and implement effectively systems that will address the cost management issues discussed in this book. The appropriate solutions can range from a low cost PC base at one extreme to the development of a company-wide information and systems strategy at the other. It is essential to the effective implementation of any solution that the approach is structured, defining the problems, specifying information requirements, designing the system, selecting the software and then moving on to implementation.

In conclusion, however, it must be emphasised that no amount of structured planning will guarantee the success of an implementation without the commitment and sponsorship of users and senior management. The focus of this book has been on managing the business through the generation and use of focused, meaningful and timely information. This can only happen if resources are devoted to the task and are supported by parties who have a critical interest in succeeding. Implementing new approaches to cost management and performance measurement is not an optional extra in today's environment; it is a critical component of any strategy to survive and succeed.

References

1 R. Kaplan (1990), The four stage model of cost systems design, *Management Accounting (USA)*, vol. 71, no. 8, pp. 22–6
2 R. Cooper (1990), Implementing an activity based cost system, *Journal of Cost Management*, vol. 4, no. 1, pp. 33–42
3 R. Kaplan (1990), speaker at *Relevance Regained*, ICM Conference, London
4 R. Cooper (1989), You need a new cost system when . . ., *Harvard Business Review*, vol. 67, no. 1, pp. 77–82

Index